W9-CIK-804

Brief Contents

www.wadsworth.com

www.wadsworth.com is the World Wide Web site for Wadsworth and is your direct source to dozens of online resources.

At *www.wadsworth.com* you can find out about supplements, demonstration software, and student resources. You can also send email to many of our authors and preview new publications and exciting new technologies.

www.wadsworth.com
Changing the way the world learns®

Writing With Style

APA Style Made Easy

3RD EDITION

LENORE T. SZUCHMAN
Barry University

THOMSON
™
WADSWORTH

Australia • Canada • Mexico • Singapore • Spain
United Kingdom • United States

Publisher/Executive Editor: Vicki Knight
Editorial Assistant: Monica Sarmiento
Marketing Manager: Dory Schaeffer
Marketing Assistant: Laurel Anderson
Advertising Project Manager: Brian Chaffee
Project Manager, Editorial Production: Cheri Palmer
Art Director: Vernon Boes
Print/Media Buyer: Judy Inouye

Permissions Editor: Stephanie Lee
Production Service: Shepherd, Inc.
Text Designer: John Edeen
Copy Editor: Kevin Campbell
Cover Designer: Kim Rokusek
Cover Image: © 2004 Rokusek Design, Inc.
Compositor: Shepherd, Inc.
Printer: Webcom

Printed in the Canada
1 2 3 4 5 6 7 08 07 06 05 04

For more information about our products,
contact us at:
**Thomson Learning Academic Resource
Center 1-800-423-0563**
For permission to use material from this text or
product, submit a request online at
http://www.thomsonrights.com.
Any additional questions about permissions can
be submitted by email to
thomsonrights@thomson.com.

Library of Congress Control Number: 2004102869

ISBN 0-534-63432-X

Wadsworth/Thomson Learning
10 Davis Drive
Belmont, CA 94002-3098
USA

Asia
Thomson Learning
5 Shenton Way #01-01
UIC Building
Singapore 068808

Australia/New Zealand
Thomson Learning
102 Dodds Street
Southbank, Victoria 3006
Australia

Canada
Nelson
1120 Birchmount Road
Toronto, Ontario M1K 5G4
Canada

Europe/Middle East/Africa
Thomson Learning
High Holborn House
50/51 Bedford Row
London WC1R 4LR
United Kingdom

Latin America
Thomson Learning
Seneca, 53
Colonia Polanco
11560 Mexico D.F.
Mexico

Spain/Portugal
Paraninfo
Calle Magallanes, 25
28015 Madrid, Spain

In memory of my parents

Contents

C H A P T E R **3**

Preparing the Introduction Section and the Literature Review Paper   28

C H A P T E R **4**

Preparing the Method Section   45

C H A P T E R **5**

Preparing the Results Section   63

CHAPTER **10**

Grooming Tips for Psychology Papers   **116**

CHAPTER **11**

Preparing a Poster Presentation   **127**

APPENDIX

Wrapping It Up   **135**

Preface

This book offers psychology students a new method for learning to write research papers in the style described in the *Publication Manual of the American Psychological Association.* It calls their attention to the style of writing used in actual professional journals and leads them through a process of collecting examples of words, phrases, and sentences that illustrate the essential stylistic components. They can use these examples in their own papers.

This book can be used in several types of classes. Ideally, it should be used early in the training of psychology majors, but after composition requirements are completed. It can be assigned as the first month's work in a writing-intensive course such as Research Methods or Experimental Psychology. It can also be used to *replace* writing requirements in lower-level content courses (such as Developmental Psychology). In this case, students can be instructed to use only journals related to the content area in their assignments. Those students will be less intimidated by assignments using journal sources in subsequent courses. If a university's program permits, this book can be used by the English composition faculty in sections designed for psychology majors.

Many beginning graduate students are also in need of the training this book provides. They might use it as a supplement in their first graduate research methods classes or upon entry into the graduate program.

Why It Is Difficult for Students to Master APA Format

American Psychological Association (APA) style writing is a skill often targeted for study in research methods classes, but psychology students are usually expected to conform to APA guidelines in all of their written work. Sometimes the transition from first-year composition classes to psychology classes leaves students confused because first-year composition classes tend to be taught with emphasis on the Modern Language Association (MLA) style. In these courses students generally learn how to write a paragraph, how to write a five-paragraph essay, how to develop a "thesis statement," and how to write a library research paper in the generic (MLA-based) style. This is a useful start, but it does not enhance students' technical writing skills as much as psychology professors would like.

Shortly after declaring a psychology major, students must master a technical writing style that often contradicts the very "laws" they have learned in their composition classes. They must learn to write using APA style, which includes not only rules made explicit in the *Publication Manual* but also other conventions that constitute the *unwritten* rules of APA style (e.g., rather than write about what other authors *said* or *believed,* concentrate on what they *found* or *reported;* do not mention the title of someone's article in a literature review; use the passive voice in certain circumstances).

In order to master this new style, students are usually instructed to purchase the *Publication Manual* and use it as a reference. However, it is difficult for the student new to the style to use the *Publication Manual* in that way. One reason may be that students have little experience reading material written in APA style at this point in their training. This workbook fills this gap.

Learning by Modeling

Completing the exercises in this book will familiarize students with APA style by a method that helps them begin to *read* APA publications. The exercises require them to scan APA journals for examples of particular rules and conventions. They then learn by modeling these techniques. The lists generated by completing the exercises in *Writing With Style* can be used as students write their own papers—all the words and phrases contained in the exercises exemplify not only APA style but also the research psychologist's tone and form. Thus, students benefit not only from the *process* of searching for examples in psychology journals but also from the *item file* they develop and can use in writing their papers and research reports.

It is daunting for the newly declared psychology major to see the *Publication Manual* and realize that all writing must conform to a style set out in what looks like a reference book rather than a style guide. In fact, the *Publication Manual* is both, but many students need help in figuring out how to use it. For example, there are some rules in the *Publication Manual* that students *must* learn, and there are others that they do not have to learn. That is, some rules must become second nature (e.g., what tense to use for the method of an experiment), while others are used only occasionally and do not have to be memorized (e.g., how to abbreviate a certain measurement). I focus on the rules that should be learned, while pointing the way to types of things that should be looked up.

Throughout this book, I call attention to the need for precision in word usage. Students new to scientific writing have not always been trained to seek the type of precision required. For example, I point out that when directing readers to consult a figure or a table, it is important to think about what verbs are possible if *table* is the subject of a sentence. Likewise, students should consider what verbs are possible when an *experiment* is the subject—experiments cannot *try* to do anything, for example.

Students should not expect this book to replace the *Publication Manual*. They should be aware that this is one of several reference books that belong near them when they write. The exercises in *Writing With Style* do not cover every writing situation described in the *Publication Manual*. After all, most of the information in the *Publication Manual* is not going to be used by any one writer. There is also a suggestion in the *Publication Manual* to consult their Web site, http://www.apastyle.org, for the latest information. Here I provide general descriptions of the desired contents of each section of the research report, and I give primary emphasis to areas that students often find most difficult. Instructors are likely to find that many of the key points in this book remind them of errors in papers they have graded.

Writing With Style will also not replace a good grammar and punctuation reference. However, I do cover some general rules both throughout the book, and especially in Chapter 10 on "Grooming Tips," because in my experience, students often require additional practice with certain basic grammar and punctuation rules. These include, for example, how to identify and avoid run-on sentences and how to use a colon. These exercises also require that they scan psychology journals to search for examples of the accurate application of rules.

Content

After Chapter 1, which offers suggestions to students about why and how to use this book, the order of the chapters is flexible. Chapter 2 contains general conventions, such as how to refer to the work of others in the body of a paper and tips for avoiding sexist language. It is general enough to have some applicability to any section of a research report. The sections themselves are covered in Chapters 3 through 9 in the order that many people write and teach them. It would not be difficult, however, to assign these chapters in some other order. Chapter 10 contains guidance on avoiding the grammar and punctuation errors commonly found in undergraduate psychology papers. This chapter can be assigned at any point in a course, but students seem to find this type of work more useful after they have attempted some writing of their own. The chapter on poster presentations is last because it is likely to be assigned only if posters themselves are assigned. Many students will nevertheless benefit from having access to this material whenever they do prepare their first posters.

The Appendix, "Wrapping It Up," contains advice on rewriting. Students often assume that proofreading and revising are the same. I make several specific suggestions here for revising. Then, I lead readers through a series of proofreading exercises directing them to rely on their word processors to spot potential problems. This material is presented as an appendix to encourage instructors to assign it whenever students prepare to turn in their first papers.

Because some students may confuse modeling and plagiarism, I include an extensive discussion of plagiarism in the first chapter. In addition, after working a few of the exercises, it becomes clear to students that many authors use similar constructions; these constructions must therefore be in the public domain. In fact, the concept of plagiarism should be more clear in the student's mind after completing this workbook than it was before.

New in the Third Edition

I have tried to keep this volume brief so that it can be used as a supplement for a variety of courses. For many courses it is likely that students will have their own copies of the *Publication Manual,* but some instructors will find that there is enough material here for students to complete assignments for certain classes without purchasing the *Publication Manual.*

The major textual additions are expanded sections on plagiarism in Chapter 1 and on the literature review in Chapter 3—with more information on the Internet in both chapters.

The most important pedagogical improvement is that in this edition most of the exercises now contain a suggested article available through InfoTrac® College Edition. Access to InfoTrac College Edition is provided with the purchase of this book, and a substantial number of APA-style publications are offered in full text through this database. My students have appreciated this addition when I tried it in my class. They report that they have more confidence in responses I have directed them to than they do in their own finds.

Acknowledgments

Many people participated in the process of preparing this book. Most important are my students and colleagues at Barry University. Frequent discussions among the psychology faculty about our students' writing led me to try new ways of introducing this material to my Experimental Psychology classes. Those students, in turn, provided feedback on my exercises through their comments and their progress. Using the second edition of this book with classes provided me insight about the ways in which it could be improved for the current edition.

I want to thank Margaret Gatz for her encouragement and kind words at the Psychology of Aging Institute at the College of St. Scholastica in Duluth. She has been generous with guidance based on her vast experience as a journal editor.

The people at Wadsworth have been great collaborators. Vicki Knight has been so supportive from the start and continues to provide common sense when I need it. I would also like to thank Monica Sarmiento, editorial assistant; Dory Schaeffer, marketing manager; Brian Chaffee, advertising project manager; Laurel Anderson, senior marketing assistant; and Cheri Palmer, production project manager for all their work on the book. Miguel Ortiz provided the initial encouragement to submit the project and remains nearby.

I also wish to thank the reviewers who made helpful suggestions for this revision: Susan Goldman, University of Illinois; Marie Huff, Western Carolina University; Gerald McRoberts, Lehigh University; and Elizabeth Soliday, Washington State University, Vancouver. Their comments and suggestions were thoughtful and practical.

Finally, no professor-wife-mother manages to complete a successful manuscript without a lot of sacrifice from husband and children. Paula and Jeff, now adult writers themselves, have begun to give collegial as well as filial support for this project. Jeff, while still in college, canvassed journals with me while I was working on the first edition. He found some of the sentences that I used as examples for these exercises and then tweaked them with his wry humor. And last is Mark, my husband, best friend, and closest colleague. He reads manuscripts, patiently reads them again, and then arranges proper settings on computer programs because form and content both count.

Lenore T. Szuchman

About the Author

Asha Fuller

Lenore T. Szuchman is a developmental psychologist who received her Ph.D. from Florida International University in 1990. In her position as professor in the Department of Psychology at Barry University, she currently teaches several writing-intensive courses, including Experimental Psychology and Advanced Experimental Psychology. She is the author and co-author of articles on social cognition in older adults. She has also supervised a wide range of master's theses and senior projects which have been presented at professional and student conferences regionally and nationally.

Dr. Szuchman majored in comparative literature at Brandeis University, where she immersed herself in great novels and mastered MLA style. She has an M.A. in special education from the University of Texas at Austin. Her teaching experience is varied, from first-grade at the American School in Buenos Aires to language arts classes in secondary school for learning disabled students in Miami, Florida. Thus, she has had rich opportunities to shape her own and her students' writing abilities.

Students in Dr. Szuchman's Experimental Psychology classes conduct six experiments and write APA-style manuscripts focusing on all but the Introduction section. In Advanced Experimental Psychology, each student develops an independent research proposal and produces a complete Introduction and Method section which often results in a senior thesis. Noticing the students' difficulties in making the transition from other types of college writing to the type required of scientific psychologists, Dr. Szuchman began to bring stacks of APA journals to class each week in her search for ways to train students to notice the differences between what they had been accustomed to reading and writing and what was now expected of them. Their valuable feedback in these classes shaped the final series of exercises produced for *Writing with Style.*

Writing With Style

APA Style Made Easy

CHAPTER 1

Introduction: The Lay People and You

You have probably enjoyed reading books found on the psychology and self-help shelves of your local bookstore. Those books may have sparked your interest in psychology and made you think you might want to study psychology in college. Those books were written to make psychology accessible to the general public. By now you should be thinking of those readers as lay people. *You are no longer among them.* You are going to become a professional. You can and should read books written for lay people, but you have to start writing like a psychologist. You stopped being one of the lay people when you finished your introductory psychology course and decided to major in psychology. You can now consider yourself a psychologist-in-training.

This book is designed to help you with the writing assignments you will face as a psychologist-in-training. The instructors who will grade your papers are accustomed to reading the articles of professional psychologists who publish in academic psychology journals. This type of writing differs from what you learned to do in English composition classes. And, as strange as it sounds, it also differs from the writing in the books you may have been reading outside of class, those that originally sparked your interest in psychology—the books you found on the psychology shelves of your local bookstore. The best of those books translate the findings of scientific psychologists into language that makes them accessible and applicable for the nonscientific reader. But you are expected to write your research papers in an entirely different fashion because your training is in scientific psychology.

Scientific Psychology

Scientific psychology is not written in the same way as pop psychology. In contrast to pop psychology, scientific psychology meets the needs of the professional psychologist. This is a person who must keep up with new findings in a very broad literature. And because of the great amount of literature produced, the more similar the format is from article to article, the more accessible it is for this type of reader. For example, the Abstract section exists to help the reader make a quick decision about whether to read the article. By providing the same type of information about every article, the abstract facilitates decisions.

The professional reads different material with different levels of attention to detail. But not all professionals read with the same focus. The reader who is highly expert in a certain area of research might be interested in the Method section of an article above all. The psychologist who is reading at the outer edge of his or her expertise might read the introduction before deciding whether to finish the article. The person who skims needs to predict where the hypotheses will be and where the most important outcome will be. Finally, a student or researcher studying the area needs to see if the reference list can point to further reading. You can see that if all parts of the article are written in a standardized way, each person's needs can be met efficiently. Sometimes this kind of writing does get repetitive for the sake of clarity, but it can still be interesting to read, and in the best examples, the prose is fluid and elegant. Certainly, one hopes that the research findings themselves generate excitement in at least a few readers. However, there can be no suspense, no teasing about the problem or its solution, no surprise endings. If generating suspense were important, the first thing to do would be to eliminate the abstract. Even topic sentences for paragraphs detract from suspense. If thrill were important, we would list results supporting the hypotheses first, and losers last (rather than list them in the sequence expected by the order of presentation of hypotheses). Surprise endings? Not for professionals; they decide whether to read a research report only after knowing how the experiment came out.

Okay, you are ready to agree that professionals need a different prose style from the one needed by lay people. But why do different professionals need different rules? Why can't everyone use MLA (Modern Language Association) or *Chicago Manual of Style* rules?

One reason is that different professions rely on different methods and different styles of argument. Scientists who do experiments *need* a different format from that of historians or literary critics. They have their own type of information to convey and their own values as consumers of their own literature. The American Psychological Association (APA) publishes many journals whose editors together consider thousands of submissions each year. The rules set forth in the *Publication Manual of the American Psychological Association,* fifth edition (2001) facilitate the handling of such a large number of manuscripts by standardizing much of the format. These rules have been so convenient for readers and writers that many other science and social science journals adhere to a similar framework.

You will certainly want to own the *Publication Manual* and use it as a reference. But a reference book is just that—use it to look things up when you are not sure of a rule. You are not expected to learn all of the rules. No psychologist submits a manuscript without looking up some rules in the *Publication Manual* along the way. Why memorize the citation format for court decisions? for reviews of videos? for a non-English chapter in an edited book? What about the rule for brackets and parentheses? Do you use brackets within parentheses or parentheses within brackets? Look it up; we all do.

Many other conventions, however, require much greater attention because you use them so often. Some of these are style rules you have encountered elsewhere, and it's time you mastered such rules as agreement of subject and verb, as well as when to use *between* versus *among.* Other conventions are unique to our field: use past tense for the results and present tense for the conclusions; abbreviate more liberally in the abstract than in the body of the paper; and use metric units whenever possible.

Unfortunately, there is more to sounding like a psychologist than following all of those rules, just as there is more to sounding like a Texan than speaking English. If you want to sound like a Texan, you have to listen to a lot of Texans talk. If you want to write like a psychologist, you have to read a lot of psychology. But you have to begin to learn to write like a psychologist before you have the opportunity to read a lot of professional psychology. This book is designed to help get you there.

How to Use This Book

This is both a rule book and a workbook. It is designed to prepare you to write your first psychology research report or to help you improve your writing after you have had a bit of experience. It will guide you through the psychological literature in a way that will focus your attention on how authors use words and phrases. It will teach you to keep lists of examples of these words and phrases so that when you write papers, you can refer to your lists for models to help you construct sentences and paragraphs of your own. This book does *not* replace the *Publication Manual.* When you write papers, you should keep both the *Publication Manual* and this filled-in workbook near you. The *Publication Manual* is your reference book; this book is your sample book. If you want to produce a sentence or a phrase in a way that will make you pass as a more experienced writer of psychology papers than you are, use your lists. If you want to find out exactly how to organize, abbreviate, or punctuate a technical section, sentence, or phrase, use the *Publication Manual.* By the way, when you use the *Publication Manual* you may worry that it sometimes seems to contradict the printed format of the journals themselves. Your papers are known as *manuscripts,* and manuscripts differ from printed material. Your responsibilities are those of the author of a manuscript, not those of a typesetter laying out pages for a journal.

You will find two types of exercises in this book. The first and most frequently presented will result in the lists of usable sentences and phrases just described. To produce these lists, use sentence frames; that is, leave blanks for the words that are specific to the research presented. For example, suppose you find the following sentence in a journal and it is an example of what you are looking for: "These findings regarding writing psychology papers have several implications." Copy it this way for your list of examples: "These findings regarding _____ have several implications." In most cases, I have sampled several journals and filled in the first few items for you with frames from my own search. Sometimes I have filled in the blanks for fun. Feel free to do the same with your own examples.

The second type of exercise is designed to help you understand a point of grammar by finding examples of it. These are found exclusively in Chapter 10, "Grooming Tips for Psychology Papers." By doing the exercises, you should learn the rules and never have to look them up again.

Your instructor may guide you to the journals you should be looking at to do the various exercises. In all cases, APA journals will be suitable. However, you should be aware that, whereas most journals specialize in empirical research articles, others (notably *Psychological Review* and *Psychological Bulletin*) publish theoretical and review articles. Unless otherwise noted, the assignments in this book require that you look at empirical research papers. Also, many important journals (e.g., *Child Development* and *Psychological Science*) are published by other organizations but adhere to APA guidelines. If your interest is primarily in one specific field of psychology, you can find out if APA guidelines are followed by a non-APA journal in the section called Instructions to Authors printed in any current edition of that journal.

If your instructor has not specified which journals to use, my advice is to sample a variety of sources. Go to your library's current periodicals area and find a single issue of five of the following journals:

Developmental Psychology

Health Psychology

Journal of Applied Psychology

Journal of Comparative Psychology

Journal of Consulting and Clinical Psychology

Journal of Experimental Psychology: Applied

Journal of Experimental Psychology: Human Perception and Performance

Journal of Experimental Psychology: Learning, Memory, and Cognition

Psychology and Aging

By sampling a range of topics, you are likely to find appropriate examples in at least one of them for any given exercise in this book.

Another alternative is to use InfoTrac® College Edition, the online library of journals. Access to this collection is provided with the purchase of this book. If you use articles from this source, note that the format is HTML rather than PDF. The PDF format exactly reproduces the articles as they appear in print, so you can trust page numbers and the look of the graphics. The HTML version contains all of the words but not the visual form of the print version. Therefore, do not assume that formatting (such as italics) is preserved. For the same reason, you will have to consult hard copies of journals when it is time to learn about tables and figures. One way to use this database for your work in this book is to click on Browse and select a few appropriate journals from the list that follows. Then you can use something general for your search term (e.g., participants, age, behavior). This should provide a list of article titles that might interest you, and you can search through some of them for the examples called for in the exercise. Alternatively, you can search by journal title using Advanced Search. Put one of those titles in and browse the titles of the articles that your search retrieves.

If you are using InfoTrac College Edition, here are some journals that you could use for many of the exercises in this book.

American Journal of Community Psychology

Archives of Sexual Behavior

British Journal of Psychology

Child Development

College Student Journal

Counseling and Values

Current Psychology

Exceptional Children

Journal of Abnormal Child Psychology

Journal of Cross-Cultural Psychology

Journal of Counseling and Development

Journal of Emotional and Behavioral Disorders

Journal of General Psychology

Journal of Genetic Psychology

Journal of Learning Disabilities

Journal of Occupational and Organizational Psychology

Journal of Sex Research

Journal of Social Psychology

Journal of Youth and Adolescence

Language and Speech

Measurement and Evaluation in Counseling and Development

Merrill-Palmer Quarterly

Personality and Social Psychology Bulletin

Research on Aging

Sex Roles: A Journal of Research

In addition to browsing, you can go to some specific articles available through InfoTrac College Edition that are suggested for completing many of the exercises in this book.

Plagiarism

Students are often surprised to learn of the variety of behaviors that constitute *plagiarism.* In fact, much of the plagiarism found among college students is unintentional. But whether or not the behavior was intentional, the penalties may be severe. With plagiarism, as with criminal law, ignorance is no excuse. By working through this book, you have committed yourself to the effort of sharpening your writing skills. Therefore, it is also a good moment to consider the variety of misdeeds that you may accidentally commit when preparing your written work in scientific psychology.

Everyone seems to know that using someone else's words without giving that author credit is unacceptable. It does not matter whether you find these words in a journal article, in a friend's term paper, or on the Internet. This rule is quite simple to follow: Use quotation marks when you are really using someone's exact words. Failing to do this is plagiarism whether or not you attribute the ideas to the proper person, because you have made it seem as if the ideas may be borrowed but the words are your own.

A lot has been written lately about how easy plagiarism has become now that students can cut and paste from the Internet. *The New York Times* (Rimer, 2003, September 3) reported on a study by Donald McCabe, a professor at Rutgers University, who found that 38% of undergraduate students said that in the last year they had done just that—cut and pasted from the Internet without citing the source. Nearly half of these students did not think that they had cheated. Perhaps this is made more appealing because much of what students find on the Internet does not seem to have an author or a date of publication. That does not mean, however, that stealing it is legal. It may mean that it has little intellectual value, and students should always be wary of using unsigned sources. But the *APA Manual* has gone to great lengths to establish formats for Internet citation. "At a minimum, a reference of an Internet source should provide a document title or description, a date (either the date of publication or update or the date of retrieval), and an address (in Internet terms, a uniform resource locator, or URL). Whenever possible, identify the authors of a document as well" (p. 269).

Often, students would like to paraphrase and give credit for the ideas, but they cannot think of original ways to express these ideas. Paraphrasing is a skill that takes some effort to acquire, so it is not surprising that when students find a useful thought in someone else's writing they are stymied about how a paraphrase can ever be better than the original. Some turn to the thesaurus to solve the problem. They leave the sentence more or less the way it is, but use a thesaurus to find words that might replace some of the words in the original author's sentence. These students assume that once they change some words, the sentence no longer requires quotation marks. Compounding this flawed strategy, they go on to think that if it does not need quotation marks, perhaps it does not even need to be credited to someone else at all. However, it is a secret little known to students that professors actually get some of their best laughs out of "thesaurus sentences."

Let me demonstrate. Here is the sentence at the end of the last paragraph after the thesaurus treatment: *It is a confidence obscure to scholars that gurus actually get their prime snorts out of thesaurus remarks.* Surely that is not what I meant to say. The fact that this does not convey the intended meaning is inconvenient, but the fact that it is still plagiarism may carry a severe penalty. In this example, the sentence *structure* has been plagiarized. You can't take someone else's sentence structure, replace a few words, and then call it your own. That's plagiarism.

There is a way to be fairly safe from unintentional plagiarism. Never try to paraphrase one sentence at a time. Instead, first read through the whole section you wish to paraphrase, then write your paraphrase, but without looking at the original. Then, be sure to credit the *ideas* conveyed in the paraphrased sections to their author. If you must quote a phrase or a sentence, do so. But don't change the original just a bit and then think it is a paraphrase. When using Internet sources, print the whole document or take notes from the screen. Don't cut and paste for later paraphrase—treat the source just as you would an article photocopied at the library. A good guideline is to "use a little and give credit" (Talub, 2000, p. 7). In fact, that is just about the same advice I could give for print sources. Once you have used a little from a lot of sources, you have transformed the material into something of your own, and you have broken no laws.

Now that you have learned to avoid stealing someone's sentence structure, what about the structure of a larger unit? Suppose you find a literature review on the same subject as your own. What is the plagiarism risk in this case? If you organize the material around the same themes as someone else, you have plagiarized. If you use the same examples to make the same point, you have plagiarized. To prevent these forms of plagiarism, consider using the reference list of a literature review to help you with your own library work, but don't read the actual review article until you have drawn some conclusions of your own. Then when you find that the review author has made a point you would like to add to your own review, you can cite that author for having had a certain insight about some research that you have also read—but that did not provide you the same insight. You can even cite the author of the literature review for finding themes in the literature that organized the topic in a useful way.

What about borrowing ideas from your professor or your textbook? To be safe, you must give credit in those cases as well. You may be expected to get your knowledge from these sources, but if you use that knowledge in a written product of your own, cite the sources. Although it may not be strictly defined as plagiarism, it is also unethical to use your own words more than once as if you had written them fresh for more than one class. Each professor expects that work written to fulfill the requirements of a certain class be submitted *only* for that class. After all, researchers are not permitted to publish the same paper in two journals. And no one is allowed to sell a product as new if it has already been used. If you have a paper already written that seems to serve the needs of another assignment, check with the second professor for guidance about how much of the paper needs to be refreshed before you recycle it for the second class.

Students sometimes have trouble deciding when a statement needs a reference and when it does not. You do not need to cite someone else for your own opinions or for generally agreed-upon facts or principles. Your own opinion is easy to identify. By contrast, at least in psychology, it is difficult to decide which facts are generally agreed upon. It is tempting to assume that everyone sees behavior exactly as you do. For example, most observers may agree that adolescence is a time when self-esteem is fragile. But wait. Are you as sure about that as you are about the fact that, in the United States, adolescents are expected to attend school? In fact, when you talk about psychological constructs like self-esteem, you are very near the divide between fact and nonfact. If you cannot find a reference for your assertion about self-esteem, at least hedge it a bit. Perhaps you can assert that there *seems* to be an emphasis in our culture on the fragility of adolescent self-esteem. If you have really searched the literature on self-esteem, then you will have references at your disposal to cite when you make an assertion. Cite them and you are safe.

Students new to a field may also be confused about when a phrase is a standard technical term and when it is an original term. You are free to use technical phrases without attribution. Usually it is safe to use effects that authors study (e.g., transfer of training) or variables they use (e.g., test anxiety) without quotation marks. If you use a short phrase that you are not sure should be attributed to an author, use no quotation marks, but do include a page reference along with the rest of the citation information.

You may have begun to wonder how you can be safe from plagiarism if you are copying sentences from published sources into this book for later use in your own papers. The reason you can do that is the same reason you can use a dictionary or a book of foreign phrases without fear of plagiarism. You need to learn how words are used before you can use them on your own. People who share a subculture, as do scholars in any discipline, tend to use words and even whole phrases in a particular way. As you do the exercises in this book, you will find that the same phrases keep appearing in the articles you scan. You may even have difficulty finding enough different examples of a given type to fill the spaces provided. As rich as the English language is, only a finite number of ways exist for phrasing a prediction or the results of a *t* test. When a form is used repeatedly, you are allowed to use it without fear that someone else "owns" it.

A lot of the discussion about plagiarism, here and in other parts of your educational experience, is presented as a series of rules you have to follow in order to avoid getting into trouble. It is important to take a moment to consider the main reason that scholars do not plagiarize. There is tremendous satisfaction in doing good research, writing good manuscripts, having original ideas, and explaining them coherently, even elegantly if possible. That satisfaction is not to be had when some part of the material or some of the ideas are stolen from someone else or when data are fabricated. Scholars in an academic field usually love their jobs and put in far more hours than would be required in most other professions. They do this because it brings them joy. My observation is that students also get great pleasure from a job well done, and that kind of pleasure does not come from claiming someone else's accomplishments as one's own.

My Style in This Book Should Not Be Your Style for a Research Report

In preparing this book I have had to consider my own role as a model for your writing. I have explained that technical writing is formal. A formal tone does not, for example, speak to the reader as "you." The articles you will read are designed to inform, not to amuse. Journal articles do not contain informal language, slang, contractions, or humor. If I were to write this book in that tone, it would be a good example for you, but it would not serve my purpose. Undoubtedly, you write differently for different purposes already. Now that you are learning the rules of a scientific style for a new purpose, I do not want you modeling your scientific prose from novels, newspapers, or textbooks—or any sources other than those specifically written in APA style. Textbooks do not necessarily benefit from such a style. Therefore, I have chosen not to conform strictly to APA style in this book. However, I hope that you will not catch me making spelling, grammar, or punctuation errors.

CHAPTER 2

Some Generalizations About How Psychologists Write

Referring to Other Authors

One of the most common topics that psychologists and psychology students write about is each other. In fact, the longest part of a published research study is usually the introduction, in which the author surveys the research that led to the current study. Advanced students and researchers often write research proposals that emphasize the same type of material found in the introductions of printed articles. Finally, undergraduate and graduate students are often assigned to write literature reviews as term papers. Therefore, it is very important to learn what the *Publication Manual* has to say about conveying the ideas and findings of other authors. Likewise, it is valuable to search some journals to see what generalizations can be made about the unwritten rules.

When you refer to the work of another author or authors, use last names only, and do not mention the titles of their works. The publication year is a necessary part of the citation, but it is seldom presented as part of the sentence. Students often write, "In 1995, Smith did a study of . . ." However, it is much more appropriate to keep the year in parentheses unless you are making a special point of the date. When referring to the same study twice within a single paragraph, do not include the year after the first instance, unless there is the possibility of confusing the reader about two studies by the same author published in different years.

▲ **REMINDER BOX** ▼

Refer to other authors by last name only and do not mention the titles of their works (except in the References section).

You have the option of inserting the author's name and year of publication in parentheses: "A study of X has revealed dramatic changes over the last decade (Smith, 1995)." If you do this, however, you *cannot* also include the author in the body of the same sentence. An example of this type of error is the following sentence: "Smith's study of X has revealed dramatic changes over the last decade (Smith, 1995)." Your best bet would be to keep the author and the year in parentheses. Normally, the point of your sentence is what the author did, not who the author is. On those rare occasions when you do wish to name a theorist or compare the work of two authors, then you can pull the name out of the parentheses and put it in the sentence.

Another problem with regard to citations is how to refer to works that you have not read. First, try to get every relevant article and read it. However, instructors understand that students are more likely than published authors to cite materials from secondary sources. Be aware that this does not allow you to put the sources you have not read yourself (primary/original sources) on your references list. Put the source you *read* in the References section. In the body of the paper, you can mention the original work and indicate that you found mention of it in a secondary source—which you *do* cite. Example: "Skinner (as cited in Smith & Jones, 2000) found no evidence of emotion in rats." Smith and Jones will be on your reference list; Skinner will not.

▲ **REMINDER BOX** ▼

If you have not read a source, do not list it in your References section. In the body of the paper, refer to the source you did read (secondary source) and indicate that the primary source was cited in the secondary source.

A potential source of confusion exists when referring to someone else's research as the "current" study, the "present" study, or "this" study. These terms always refer to the study reported in the Method and Results sections of the article you are reading (or the research report you are writing). When you are looking at an article and writing about the outcome of that author's study in your own paper, you may come across one of these phrases, and it may find its way into your description of that study. Do not do it. You may confuse your readers even more than this paragraph has confused you! And for the same reason.

▲ REMINDER BOX ▼

Do not use "the current study" or "the present study" to refer to someone else's work.

One charming feature of our profession is that psychologists are very polite when disagreeing with or disapproving of colleagues. You should be sensitive to this tone in your own reviews of the literature. A psychologist who feels that Smith has done a terrible study may only say, "Other researchers have failed to replicate Smith's result." Or, "Smith may have failed to take into account the . . ." Also be careful about your tone when describing a controversial issue. Present both sides and indicate what kind of data support one conclusion and what kind support the other.

Words and Phrases to Collect

The English language contains so many words and expressions that it may come as a surprise to learn how often psychologists stick to the same ones over and over again. This is actually of benefit to the new writer because with a collection of stock words and phrases, anyone can *sound* like a psychologist even while still learning to *think* like one. In this section you will create a collection of some of these words and phrases to sprinkle in your own writing.

First, consider how often sentences in a literature review are constructed around a researcher or a research study as the grammatical subject. For example, "Smith and Jones (2001) demonstrated that . . ." You may be tempted to vary your sentences, choosing the author sometimes, the research study at other times. Be cautious about this. You are obligated to use verbs that logically suit the abilities of your grammatical subjects. People are capable of many activities (verbs), but experiments can hardly *do* anything. Consider this problem whenever you are tempted to begin a sentence with "The study . . ." Exactly what can a study do?

Exercise 1

Select several articles that cover topics of interest to you or that have been assigned in your course. Find verbs in which the grammatical subject of a sentence is someone's *study, work, experiment, research.* It may also be useful to include the object of that verb.

> *Find the answer using InfoTrac College Edition:* Araya, T., Akrami, N., & Ekehammar, B. (2003). Forgetting congruent and incongruent stereotypical information. *The Journal of Social Psychology, 143,* 433–449.

1. employs methods
2. demonstrates
3. provides evidence

4. _____

5. _____

6. _____

7. _____

8. _____

9. _____

Another nonhuman grammatical subject often found in research reports is the outcome of someone's research. The words to look for here are *findings, results, evidence.* Don't be surprised if the list you create for this exercise has a lot of overlap with the previous one.

Exercise 2

List the verbs in sentences in which the subject is some kind of experimental *outcome.*

> *Find the answer using InfoTrac College Edition:* Kochenderfer-Ladd, B. (2003). Identification of aggressive and asocial victims and the stability of their peer victimization. *Merrill-Palmer Quarterly, 49,* 401–425.

1. demonstrates

2. can be explained

3. suggests

4. _____

5. _____

6. _____

7. _____

8. _____

9. _____

10. _____

What can theories do? What can be done to them?

Exercise 3

Find the verbs or verb phrases that are used with *theories* or *hypotheses*.
Find the answer using InfoTrac College Edition: Maticka-Tyndale, E., Herold, E. S., & Oppermann, M. (2003.) Casual sex among Australian schoolies. *The Journal of Sex Research, 40,* 158–170.

1. take something as evidence

2. have been challenged

3. focus on

4. lead to the hypothesis that

5. _____

6. _____

7. _____

8. _____

9. _____

10. _____

You may have noticed in completing the previous three exercises that authors often use passive verb constructions when discussing a study, an outcome, or a theory. For example, they will note that a study was *designed* for some purpose. That type of writing shows you that the author knows that studies themselves can't assess or find or test. Authors design studies so that they (the authors) can assess things.

In contrast to inanimate studies and abstractions such as theories, a researcher or group of researchers can very easily be the grammatical subject of a sentence. In this case, look for sentences in which the subject is a specific author or authors, or a more general noun such as *author, researcher,* or *experimenter.*

Exercise 4

List the verbs associated with *researchers.* (Here you have been given plenty of space for a long list.) When you find a word more than once, put a check mark next to it every time you find it.

 Find the answer using InfoTrac College Edition: Cemalcilar, Z., Canbeyli, R., & Sunar, D. (2003). Learned helplessness, therapy, and personality traits: An experimental study. *The Journal of Social Psychology, 143,* 65–81.

1. have shown

2. found

3. replicated

4. reported

5. _____

6. _____

7. _____

8. _____

9. _____

10. _____

11. _____

12. _____

13. _____

14. _____

15. _____

16. _____

17. _____

18. _____

19. _____

20. _____

▲ REMINDER BOX ▼

Use a person (e.g., "the researcher" or a proper name) rather than a product (e.g., study, experiment, or finding) as a sentence subject whenever possible.

Now that you know 20 things that psychologists *do,* please take note of the words you did NOT find. You probably did not find *feel.* Research studies cannot feel, and researchers keep their feelings to themselves. Also, you probably found less thinking and believing than you might have expected. Perhaps *believe* doesn't convey the scientific attitude as well as the word *hypothesize* does. Likewise, researchers very often *reason,* but it seems as if they hardly ever *think.* Another type of word that will be rare on your lists is related to writing and talking: *stated, wrote, said.* Journalists report what people say and write. Psychologists use the writings of others to report what they found or investigated.

▲ REMINDER BOX ▼

Do not indicate what researchers thought, felt, believed, or said.

Another type of verb that psychologists use can be categorized as a "hedge word." We hedge even when we hold strong opinions about why people behave as they do, because usually we cannot be absolutely sure of cause and effect. Even the most carefully designed experiments do not provide ironclad evidence so that we can generalize with absolute certainty about behavior. Therefore, we avoid using confident language (e.g., the kind you just read in the previous sentence) when we are making claims about behavior. *May* and *might* are our primary hedge words: certain functions *may* decline with age; it *may* be fruitful to consider *x* in the context of *y*. Sometimes we hedge outside of the verb phrase; for example, "One possible interpretation is . . ." Also, don't forget that hypothesis testing is another excuse for a hedge word. For example, results *support* a hypothesis; they seldom *confirm* it; and they NEVER *prove* it.

Exercise 5

List some *hedges* from your articles.

Find the answer using InfoTrac College Edition: Sagarin, B. J., Rhoads, J. V. L., & Cialdini, R. B. (1998). Deceiver's distrust: Denigration as a consequence of undiscovered deception. *Personality and Social Psychology Bulletin, 24,* 1167–1176.

1. suggests

2. appears to

3. is consistent with

4. _____

5. _____

6. _____

7. _____

8. _____

9. _____

10. _____

Transition words and phrases help connect the discussion of one study to that of another. They also guide the reader through the logic of the sequence of paragraphs. They can make your writing more precise. Look for them at the beginning of sentences, set off by commas.

Exercise 6

List transition words and phrases. These are often at the beginning of sentences, but other words can hold that place as well. When you find a word or phrase at the beginning of a paragraph set off by a comma from the rest of the sentence, ask yourself if it helps connect that sentence to the previous paragraph. If it does, put it on this list.

 Find the answer using InfoTrac College Edition: Bauman, S., Adams, J. H., & Waldo, M. (2001). Resilience in the oldest-old. *Counseling and Human Development, 34,* 1–19.

1. Notably,

2. In contrast,

3. Similarly,

4. _____

5. _____

6. _____

7. _____

8. _____

9. _____

10. _____

A common mistake is using a transition by itself (such as *on the other hand*) that requires the explicit use of a preceding one (*on one hand*). Also, if you are going to enumerate your points, use *first, second, third*–NOT *firstly, secondly, thirdly.* And don't use *second* if you haven't been explicit about *first.*

Words and Phrases to Avoid

The *Publication Manual* offers many examples of writing errors to avoid. This section merely highlights some common student bloopers. It would be wise for you also to look over the chapter entitled "Expressing Ideas and Reducing Bias in Language" in the *Publication Manual.*

First, Don't Forget the "No-Nos" We've Already Covered

1. Don't use the *current* or *present* study when referring to someone else's work in your literature review.

2. Don't mention authors' first names.

3. Don't provide the titles of articles you discuss in your literature review. They belong only in the References section.

4. Don't use the word *prove.* (Substitute the word *support.*)

5. Don't fool yourself into thinking you know the feelings and thoughts of the researchers you cite.

6. Don't refer to what other authors *stated, said,* or *wrote.*

Wordiness and Redundancy

Wordiness and redundancy are not the same. You should avoid using more words than you need (for example, *based on the fact that* is not as efficient as *because*), and you should also try not to say the same thing twice (e.g., *could be perhaps because* is not as good as *could be because*). Your main concern, however, is to eliminate *all* unnecessary words. Don't bother doing this until you have completed the drafts related to organization and clarity. But, by the time you are on your third or fourth draft (I realize that I'm asking you to commit yourself to quite a few drafts!), look for words you can cross out without changing any meanings. Here are examples:

1. *The results revealed that* . . . Omit the entire phrase and start your sentence with the word that would come next.

2. *The obtained data showed* . . . Where else would data come from if it had not been obtained by someone? Just say *The data showed* . . .

3. *Participants for the study were* . . . Of course they were for the study. Just say *Participants were* . . .

4. *Due to the fact that* . . . Just say *Because* . . .

5. *The reason is because* . . . Just say *The reason is* . . . The same goes for *the reasons behind why* . . .

6. *A total of eight participants* . . . Just say *Eight participants* . . .

7. *The results were statistically significant.* This is science you are reporting. Of course you are using *significant* in its statistical sense. Omit *statistical.*

8. . . . *has been previously found.* Past tense verb, so it must have occurred previously. Omit *previously.*

9. *In his study, Smith found* . . . Of course that's where he found it. Omit *In his study.*

10. *Distinctly different* . . . Choose one.

11. *Memory recall* . . . Choose one.

Overreliance on Passive Voice

The *Publication Manual* is more relaxed about allowing passive constructions than some other style manuals are. But sometimes writers get so tangled up in sentences that they don't realize that changing to the active voice can be really easy. Common examples are:

1. *Participants were administered a questionnaire (drug, test, interview, and so on).* Examiners can administer tests. But as a result, *tests* are administered, not participants. What do participants do? They *take* a test. They *fill in* or *complete* a questionnaire.

2. *The experiment was designed by Smith to* . . . This type of construction is easy to turn into the active voice: *Smith designed an experiment to* . . .

Informal Language and Slang

The tone of technical writing is not colloquial—that is, it is not conversational or informal. The *Publication Manual* provides the example of *write up,* which is an informal, perhaps imprecise, way of saying *report.* Slang is the most informal type of language. Examples include the use of *blooper* to mean *error* and *no-no* to mean *something that is forbidden* (notice, my use of these words is legal—I am not writing a research report). Students usually know that slang is a *no-no,* and they avoid that type of *blooper.* But you must be on the lookout (that is, *search*) for informal language in your technical writing.

1. *Contractions are absolutely illegal.* Use apostrophes only to indicate possession. Remember that when pronouns contain possessive meanings they do so without apostrophes (e.g., *its, hers*).

2. Do not be afraid to use *because. Because* is a lovely, precise word. *Being that* is a poor replacement. *Since* is specifically made illegal for this purpose in the *Publication Manual. Since* is used to mean *after that time.*

3. Use *while* (like *since*) in its temporal sense only. Hunt for *while* in your papers. If you can't substitute *simultaneously,* perhaps you should consider *although* or *whereas.*

4. Do not be afraid to use *and.* Indulge yourself. *And* is often the best substitute for *while.* See how many wordy phrases you can kill by replacing them with *and.*

Long Quotations and Frequent Short Quotations

Because we strive for clarity and economy of expression, seldom is there need for a long quotation. Literary criticism, by contrast, would be nowhere without the long quotation. The way someone else says something is vital to what literary critics have to say about it. But technical styles are seldom quotable. If you are reporting on someone else's research, just summarize the author's point. Perhaps the author has used a word in a new way; if so, place quotation marks around that word. The *Publication Manual* has a rule about how to cite page numbers when quoting from another's work (in parentheses after the close quotation mark), and special rules about indenting long quotations (indent the entire quotation 1.2 inches from the left). You should use the indented form only for long passages (40 or more words), for example, when you are quoting from your own experimental materials or instructions to participants. See Chapter 8 for more information on quotation format.

It is easy to sympathize with someone who would like to avoid plagiarism and avoid short quotations at the same time. Sometimes you may feel that there is no efficient way to convey the contents of a certain phrase (e.g., "responses were scored for speed and accuracy") except in the author's words. One way to solve this is to take a stretch and get a drink of water when you feel a short quotation coming on. Then when you sit down to write again, write that sentence without looking at the source. If it still comes out very close to the original, you can put the page reference in at the end of the paraphrase.

▲ REMINDER BOX ▼
Avoid long quotations and frequent brief quotations.

The Editorial We

Students are often taught (in classes other than psychology classes) that the use of *I* is to be avoided and that one alternative is to refer to yourself in the third person: the author. In psychology papers, however, that is absolutely out of the question. What remains is to refer to yourself as *we.* This is called the "editorial we." (As distinguished from the "royal we," which kings and queens use to refer to themselves.) It is common in some styles to use the editorial *we,* but the *Publication Manual* expressly advises against it. You are allowed to use *we* to refer to yourself as author, however, if your paper has more than one author. Also, you are perfectly within your rights to use *I* in a psychology paper. If that bothers you, feel free to design the sentence some other way. Sometimes the passive voice can be used instead, but usually with less than optimal results: "It was hypothesized that . . ."

The best solution is to take yourself right out of the sentence: "The hypothesis was . . ." In general, you should try to place yourself in the background of the narrative. After all, it's not about you. The emphasis should be on your ideas, your findings, the participants, and so on. When you discuss other authors, this point of view comes naturally. When you discuss what *you* did, it becomes more difficult. You will find more suggestions about how to focus away from yourself in Chapter 4 on the Method section.

▲ REMINDER BOX ▼
Do not refer to yourself as "we."

The Use of You

Do not affect a tone that implies an interaction with the reader. In a research report there is never a reason to refer to the reader of the work (as I have done throughout this textbook).

Neither is it permitted to use the word *you* instead of *one* in speaking of a hypothetical person. For example, "When you reach middle age, your vision and hearing have already begun to decline." This should be written in the third person: "When one reaches middle age, one's vision and hearing have already begun to decline." Very often, sentences containing *you* should be rewritten without reference to anyone: "By middle age, vision and hearing have already begun to decline."

▲ REMINDER BOX ▼
Do not call the reader "you."

The One-Sentence Paragraph

This is a rule you learned many years ago and should not give up now. The style you are trying to achieve is crisp, clear, and well organized. Therefore, it is likely that putting a topic sentence at the beginning of every paragraph will enhance the effect. Putting such a sentence elsewhere in the paragraph (as you may have been encouraged to do previously for the sake of variety) detracts from the goal. If you find you have written a one-sentence paragraph, you must evaluate the organizational plan that allowed that to happen. What is the topic of this paragraph? Is this sentence a topic sentence that would benefit from further elaboration? If so, perhaps you forgot to elaborate. Is your single sentence really a bit of elaboration that belongs elsewhere (for example, tied to a topic that already has its own paragraph)? If so, then move it. Is it by itself because it is actually all you really know about that subject? Perhaps your paper would be improved if you omitted material you know so little about.

▲ REMINDER BOX ▼

Start every paragraph with a topic sentence and never write one-sentence paragraphs.

Overstatement

It is very tempting to fall into this habit. When you write that "it is absolutely essential" that a certain type of study be done, that is an exaggeration, isn't it? You are probably not looking at an "enormous" problem in our society, either. Nor is a scientific report the place to discuss the "tragedy" of AIDS. On some level, all of those statements might be correct, but they are not found in professional journals.

Sexist Language

You probably know that it is no longer acceptable to use *he* when you are referring to a person who might be male or female. The *Publication Manual* advises that you not use the unpronounceable combination form *s/he* or *(s)he*. It is also not acceptable to alternate *he* and *she* as if either form could be used generically. You may use *he or she,* but sentences become unnecessarily cumbersome when you do: "The participant filled out his or her questionnaire using his or her code number."

Of the various alternatives, try to find one that eliminates the need for the singular pronoun completely. Using *his or her* every time you find that you need a possessive is not as convenient as using *their*. However, be sure that you have used a plural noun prior to replacing it with a plural pronoun. It is a common error to begin the sentence with an individual and then talk about *their score*. If you begin with one person, you must then refer to *his or her score*. The solution is to begin with the plural (people, participants, students, etc.) and then discuss *their scores*. You have thereby avoided both sexist language and an inappropriate pronoun. For the preceding example, the best solution would be: "Participants filled out their questionnaires using their code numbers."

▲ **REMINDER BOX** ▼

Do not write *he* when you mean *he or she*.

Using Prefixes as If They Were Words

A few prefixes are used quite often in psychology papers. They include *non, pre, post,* and *sub.* Please remember that prefixes cannot stand alone with spaces on both sides. They must be attached to words. They may be attached with hyphens or just stuck onto the root words, and the *Publication Manual* will guide you if you are not sure in a given case. But you can be very sure that if they stand alone, you have made a mistake. If you test nonsmokers and smokers in your experiment, be sure that you have not written *non smokers* instead of *nonsmokers*.

A general rule in APA style is that most prefixes do not take hyphens. Sometimes that makes words seem odd (like *posttest*), so be prepared. The only prefix we use frequently that *does* take a hyphen is *self.* So enjoy having self-esteem, doing self-scoring, and being self-conscious. And get used to subtest scores, reexamining the findings, interracial dyads, and intertrial intervals.

There are also some extra reasons for hyphens with prefixes. Ones you might need are the following: if the base word is capitalized (*mini-Pavlovian*), if it is a number (*pre-1957*), or if it is an abbreviation (*non-PTSD group*).

▲ **REMINDER BOX** ▼

Do not leave prefixes hanging loose from words.

Incorrect Plurals

Many professors will be annoyed if you do not use the following plurals correctly: *data, criteria, phenomena, stimuli,* and *hypotheses.* The singular forms are *datum, criterion, phenomenon, stimulus,* and *hypothesis.* You will probably never need to use *datum,* but try learning the other four right now. And please remember to use the plural verb form when you use plural nouns (e.g., data *were* gathered, the hypotheses *were* supported).

▲ REMINDER BOX ▼

These words are plural nouns: *data, criteria, phenomena, stimuli,* and *hypotheses.*

Mixed-Up Latin Abbreviations

You probably find yourself writing *et al., i.e.,* and *e.g.* a lot now. But where do the periods and commas really go? The commas go after *i.e.* and *e.g.* every time you write them. What about the periods? The periods go after abbreviations. Here's what these three abbreviations mean:

1. *Et al.* stands for *et alia,* which means "and other things." If you remember that *et* is not an abbreviation but rather a Latin word meaning "and," then you will remember that there is no reason to put a period after it. By contrast, *al.* is an abbreviation, and so it requires a period.

2. *I.e.* stands for *id est,* the Latin phrase meaning "that is." Both letters in this Latin abbreviation are legitimate abbreviations, and so they both take periods. If you need this phrase, use the Latin abbreviation inside parentheses and the English phrase "that is" outside parentheses. Either way, they are followed by a comma.

3. *E.g.* stands for *exempli gratia,* the Latin phrase meaning "for example." As with *i.e.,* these letters are both abbreviations, and so both take periods. Also, as above, if you use the phrase inside parentheses, use the Latin abbreviation, and outside the parentheses use the English equivalent. Either way, follow it with a comma.

▲ REMINDER BOX ▼

Learn how to punctuate *i.e., e.g.,* and *et al.*

CHAPTER 3

Preparing the Introduction Section and the Literature Review Paper

The APA *Publication Manual* directs that the introduction should contain five components:

1. scholarly review of relevant literature
2. purpose of the study
3. theoretical implications
4. definitions of variables
5. statement of hypotheses and their rationales

You will find that authors are often explicit about these items. An article may even begin with the words, "The purpose of the study was . . ." The final paragraphs of the introduction may contain sentences that begin with, "The specific hypotheses were . . ." And in between, you will find the literature review and theoretical implications of the current study.

By the way, you are not allowed to use the word *Introduction* as a heading for this section. The *Publication Manual* instructs that you *not* label this section in your own paper. Its location indicates what section it is. In the publications themselves, however, sometimes the word

Introduction does appear as a heading. Remember that the *Publication Manual* is directing authors of manuscripts, not printers of journals.

▲ REMINDER BOX ▼

The Introduction section does not include the label "Introduction."

What Was Done and Why

Looking a little more closely, the *Publication Manual* advises that the first paragraph or two should provide "a firm sense of what was done and why" (p. 11).

Exercise 1

Select several articles from a variety of journals or use articles that have been assigned by your professor. Examining only the first two paragraphs of your research articles, copy the single sentence in each that states the purpose of the study. If you do not find such a sentence, try the last two paragraphs of the introduction.

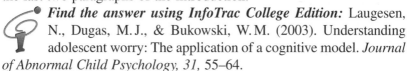 *Find the answer using InfoTrac College Edition:* Laugesen, N., Dugas, M. J., & Bukowski, W. M. (2003). Understanding adolescent worry: The application of a cognitive model. *Journal of Abnormal Child Psychology, 31,* 55–64.

1. Accordingly, the primary purpose of our study is to reexamine the findings of Lector (1999), taking into consideration the number of hours of food deprivation.

2. This research was conducted to determine variables that characterize beach umbrella dealers who show escalation in rude behavior during the winter months.

3. Elephants are always larger than turtles. In the present study we attempted to find a possible explanation for this striking finding.

4. _____

   _____

5. _____

   _____

6. _____

_____

Exercise 2

Still looking only at the first or last few paragraphs, find and copy sentences that indicate why this is an important research issue.

> **Find the answer using InfoTrac College Edition:** Fritzley, V. H., & Lee, K. (2003). Do young children always say yes to yes–no questions? A metadevelopmental study of the affirmation bias. *Child Development, 74,* 1297–1313.

Also this one: Araya, T., Akrami, N., & Ekehammar, B. (2003). Forgetting congruent and incongruent stereotypical information. *The Journal of Social Psychology, 143,* 433–449.

1. Knowledge of these factors may help identify individuals at risk for . . .

2. The problem under study here has been implicated in many psychological theories as vitally important to the functioning of . . .

3. As knowledge of the consequences of *x* has increased, investigators have become interested in . . .

4. _____

_____

5. _____

_____

6. _____

_____

Now consider how authors introduce their work. The first sentence of an article is always written with some strategy in mind. The author might want to demonstrate the importance of the issue or the purpose at the start. Or there might be other attention-grabbing ways to begin. But this is the place to beware of the temptation to overstate, as noted in Chapter 2. Assume that the reader is trained in the general area of psychology you are writing about. For example, you do not need to note that health psychologists have long researched unhealthy behaviors and so it is important to study smoking cessation. They also know that lots and lots of people smoke, so it is not necessary to attempt the journalistic technique of telling the reader just how many there are. More appropriate would be to note that despite great efforts at research about smoking and at the implementation of smoking cessation programs, some percentage of people continue to smoke. That is the sort of fact that would interest a psychologist more than the number of people who smoke.

Exercise 3

Copy the first sentence from several articles. Indicate what type of information it contains. It is possible that some of the sentences you found for the previous two exercises held this place of honor in an article. For this exercise, however, don't recycle specific sentences from the previous exercises.

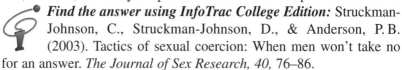 ***Find the answer using InfoTrac College Edition:*** Struckman-Johnson, C., Struckman-Johnson, D., & Anderson, P. B. (2003). Tactics of sexual coercion: When men won't take no for an answer. *The Journal of Sex Research, 40,* 76–86.

Also this one: Bosco, S. M., & Harvey, D. (2003). Effects of terror attacks on employment plans and anxiety levels of college students. *College Student Journal, 37,* 438–446.

1. A growing body of literature indicates that interactions with their owners can have a critical impact on the well-being of pets. (A statement of a long-studied problem)

2. Given the paucity of information on [my topic] and the strong impact it has on [something the reader is concerned about], this study examined [something that has not been, but should be studied].

3. Fear of death can be defined as . . . (A definition)

4. Elderly male residents of assisted living facilities who still maintain their ability to drive at night are very popular indeed. (A statement of a well-known phenomenon)

5. Persons over the age of 110 often flood counseling centers with their marital problems. (Alarming but little-known statistics)

6. _____

   _____

7. _____

   _____

8. _____

   _____

Exercise 4

Now look at the final few paragraphs of the introduction. Find the specific hypotheses. Copy the phrases that indicate that these are *hypotheses*. Look for such words as *predict* or *expect* if you don't see what you are looking for right away.

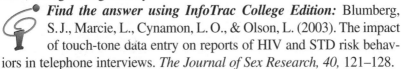 ***Find the answer using InfoTrac College Edition:*** Blumberg, S. J., Marcie, L., Cynamon, L. O., & Olson, L. (2003). The impact of touch-tone data entry on reports of HIV and STD risk behaviors in telephone interviews. *The Journal of Sex Research, 40,* 121–128.

1. Specific predictions were as follows . . .
2. Experience with vegetables should affect the way in which babies understand differences between peas and carrots.
3. The use of hot peppers was expected to enhance the flavor of the pizza.

4. _____

5. _____

6. _____

    Hypotheses need rationales—they are not supposed to be based on intuition or hunches. It is possible that early on in the research process, an experimenter did have a hunch. That hunch may even have led the researcher to begin the project, perhaps by beginning a literature search to support that hunch. By the time the literature has been reviewed, the author is supposed to be able to support the hypotheses with something more convincing than his or her original hunch. Researchers normally use previous results or theories to predict how they expect an experiment to come out. When writing your hypothesis, you are expected to provide the reasons why, for example, one group will score higher than another, or why one manipulation will yield overestimations and another will yield underestimations of a measured weight. This process is implicit in the entire literature review contained in the introduction. But it is good practice to make these reasons explicit at the point where the hypotheses are discussed.

Exercise 5

Find examples of rationales for hypotheses. Some articles will not provide these in an explicit way just prior to or just after hypotheses have been stated. Do not use those articles for this exercise. Find some examples of explicit rationales only.

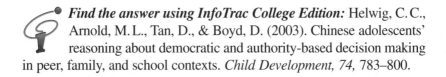 ***Find the answer using InfoTrac College Edition:*** Helwig, C. C., Arnold, M. L., Tan, D., & Boyd, D. (2003). Chinese adolescents' reasoning about democratic and authority-based decision making in peer, family, and school contexts. *Child Development, 74,* 783–800.

1. If there are qualitative differences between the common cold and the Ebola virus, differences in their effects on behavior could be expected.

2. From prior research with various primate groups, cognitively based grooming strategies were expected to be evident in humans.

3. Because our prior analysis pointed to the importance of avoiding alcohol when driving, . . .

4. _____

_____

5. _____

_____

6. _____

_____

Note that hypotheses often state a direction. That is, they make predictions that one group will perform better than another rather than just perform differently. In Example 3, it might be expected specifically that the alcohol-impaired drivers would not drive as well as the unimpaired group—not simply that one group (unspecified) would not drive as well as the other. When hypotheses do not contain a predicted direction of effect, they are sometimes called *research questions.* For example, a researcher might wish to compare two types of support groups without a firm belief that one is better than the other. Sometimes these studies are called *descriptive.* In such cases, researchers want to learn *how* groups differ before they attempt to explain the reason or the mechanism for the difference. Another type of study may be designed so that one outcome would support one hypothesis and a different outcome would support a competing hypothesis. The research question would be posed in terms indicating which one of the two theories explaining a given phenomenon is more likely to be correct.

Exercise 6

Find examples of research questions. These are likely to be signaled by such words as *describe, explore,* and *assess.*

> *Find the answer using InfoTrac College Edition:* Fleishman, J. A., Sherbourne, C. D., Cleary, P. D., Wu, A. W., Crystal, S., & Hays, R. D. (2003). Patterns of coping among persons with HIV infection: Configurations, correlates, and change. *American Journal of Community Psychology, 32,*187–204.

> *Or try this one—it tests two conflicting hypotheses:* Else-Quest, N. M., Shibley Hyde, J., & Clark, R. (2003). Breastfeeding, bonding, and the mother–infant relationship. *Merrill-Palmer Quarterly,* 49, 495–521.

1. The present study investigated relations between Measure A and Measure B, indexing two dimensions of . . .

2. We asked whether [this] and [that] explain differences between two groups of individuals.

3. The present study is designed to assess the role of love relationships in the life of one-celled organisms. Lack of such data represents an important gap in the literature.

4. _____

_____

5. _____

_____

6. _____

_____

In trying to provide "a firm sense of what was done and why," writers sometimes have difficulty deciding how much methodological detail is appropriate in the introduction. You should find statements referring to the method of the study being reported. Authors use *the current study* or *the present study* to distinguish their own from the others mentioned in the literature review. (Be careful NOT to use these words in your own literature review except to refer to the study you are either proposing or whose results you are reporting.) Notice what issues of methodology the authors highlight in the introduction. They may try to distinguish the special nature of a control group, the elimination of a confound they have discovered in previous studies similar to their own, or some innovation they are contributing.

Exercise 7

Copy the phrases or sentences found toward the end of the introduction that signal information about methodology. Search only in Introduction sections, not Method sections.

 Find the answer using InfoTrac College Edition: Robinson, E. J., & Whitcombe, E. L. (2003). Children's suggestibility in relation to their understanding about sources of knowledge. *Child Development, 74,* 48–62.

1. We modified the standard procedure for measuring shoe-size variability by presenting . . .

2. Because the ranking procedures used by Smith (1989) favored women, we offset this bias by . . .

3. Participants were required to read vignettes varying in degree of . . .

4. _____

5. _____

6. _____

The final few paragraphs should also define variables and indicate how you have operationalized your definitions. This applies to both dependent and independent variables. You may have used an established procedure, or you may need to explain briefly your own method.

Exercise 8

Find and copy examples of definitions of variables.

 Find the answer using InfoTrac College Edition (look for the term "conceptualized"): Wilson, B. A., Holm, J. E., & Bishop, K. L. (2002). Predicting responses to sexually aggressive stories: The role of consent, interest in sexual aggression, and overall sexual interest. *The Journal of Sex Research, 39,* 275–283.

1. Babies were classified according to thumb-sucking categories using the thumb-sketch method.

2. Sense of humor was measured by Curly and Moe's (1968) Laugh Scale.

3. Attractiveness was measured by participants' ratings of the photographs on a 9-point scale.

4. _____

5. _____

6. _____

Literature Review

Before we begin this section, let's take the opportunity to notice that a literature review can be published as such, and there are journals devoted to literature reviews, such as *Review of General Psychology, Psychological Review,* and *Psychological Bulletin.* Students are often asked to write papers based on library research rather than on laboratory research, and these are also literature reviews. A section at the end of this chapter is devoted to this type of review.

When you prepare a literature review either for its own sake or as part of the introduction to a research report, you will first want to consult an electronic database, and most psychologists start with PsychINFO. Recall the difference between you and the lay people that I stressed in Chapter 1. Your new professional persona requires that you use only certain types of sources for your literature review: peer-reviewed sources. You cannot generally cite items from the popular press or from the Internet. The Internet sometimes does contain appropriate sources, but doing a Google search is going to waste your time. If you don't believe it, stop right now and do a Google search for *adolescence* and *self-esteem.* The first page of my search turned up an unsigned article on a religious site, a student newsletter article (signed), a list of thesis titles at Hong Kong University, the name of a counselor who can help empower me, and a fact sheet published in Calgary. I could have spent the same time checking PsychINFO and been assured that all articles, book chapters, and books from this database are legitimate sources for a psychology paper.

You will do a keyword search and read many abstracts before deciding which articles to look at for information relevant to your topic. You are looking for theories about your topic, findings relevant to your topic, methodology used to study your topic, and literature reviews about your topic. You won't be able to locate all of the sources you would like to read in your library or through your library's full-text databases. If you have the time, you might want to use interlibrary loan. But at some point, you will say, "Enough!" And you will read and take notes on articles to which you do have access. (Please do take notes. Hot pink highlighting provides a certain aesthetic pleasure, but when it is time to begin writing, notes are much more useful.)

For a research report, the rule given by the *Publication Manual* says, "Discuss the literature but do not include an exhaustive historical review" (p. 16). Students, however, are usually held to a different standard: They will need to communicate to their instructor that they have read *and understood* other research articles in the related area. To do this, they will need to provide more detail about the studies they review than do authors of the studies reviewed. You can still be selective about what *kind* of detail you provide.

Each study cited in your literature review is cited for a specific purpose. For example, you may want to stress method in one and findings in another. You should not summarize exhaustively every study in your review. However, you will need to provide a paragraph or two on those studies even though the published articles only offer a sentence or two about relevant research studies.

When you attempt to summarize the method of a published study that contains several conditions or several similar experiments with small variations, concentrate on one experiment or condition and describe it clearly. Then you will be able to mention the variations very briefly and they will be clear (Bem, 1995). For example, for a vignette study, you might describe one of the vignettes and then explain that the other groups read vignettes that varied the age of the protagonist or the number of years of experience of the fictional job applicant. For a study of instructional methods, describe one method, the tasks, and the dependent measure. Then you can briefly note that other groups were identical except for the instructional methods—which you then describe.

It is not usually desirable to note that there were several experiments reported and then to describe each one. Describe the general method only. Then, as with the description of various groups, you can explain how the variations on the method were accomplished. When you describe results after using this technique for describing the method, you will find it easy to compare the results for each group or experimental variation at the end of your paragraph.

After gathering all your notes, it is time to organize them for the review. Keep in mind the point you are making about each study. This will help you introduce the paragraph containing the details. There should be some evidence of linear logic in the introduction, but students sometimes find themselves without good reasons for sequencing a particular set of studies. When this happens, they introduce paragraphs with phrases like, "Smith (1995) found that . . ." or "Smith (1995) also did a study of . . ." But this type of writing introduces a common problem: failing to show the connections among the studies in the review. Thus, *also* is not always a good term to link studies together. But you might want to make the point that the two researchers did something very similar. Perhaps you have decided to build a case for someone's theory by adding more evidence. If this is true, then say so. Alternatively, you might prefer to emphasize that this study appears similar to another, but an important difference remains and you want to explain it. Knowing *why* you are including a particular study will give you a much better idea of *where* to include it. In this way, your paragraphs will begin with more natural transitions and have appropriately clear topic sentences. Once again, keep in mind that your own literature review will contain more details than are included in the articles you read. It is time now to take a look at these types of transitions.

Exercise 9

Copy phrases that introduce the discussion of specific studies under review. Look particularly for words or phrases that serve as markers for the author's organizational plan.

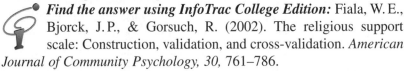 *Find the answer using InfoTrac College Edition:* Fiala, W. E., Bjorck, J. P., & Gorsuch, R. (2002). The religious support scale: Construction, validation, and cross-validation. *American Journal of Community Psychology, 30,* 761–786.

1. In line with these findings . . .

2. Another puzzling aspect of memory is . . .

3. Although Smith's (2001) findings are clear and consistent, Jones (2000) has pointed out . . .

4. The results of *x* are consistent with *y.*

5. Smith (1995) developed a system for classifying aspects of the phenomenon identified by Jones (1994).

6. According to Smith (1995), children who have the strongest attachments to their pets . . .

7. Another kind of research tactic has been to . . .

8. _____

9. _____

10. _____

11. _____

12. _____

13. _____

14. _____

15. _____

Your literature review is *not* the place for your opinions. If you find the sample in an experiment to be very small, you can only call attention to that fact if someone else has found different results with a similar but larger sample. Perhaps the author has noted a problem in his or her own Discussion section; if so, you then have tacit permission to cite the author's own misgivings. You may speculate about contradictory findings, but, once again, be careful not to be critical of the work of either author. Try not to write about what authors *did not* do unless you are contrasting it with what you are about to do or with what someone else did. For example, Smith may not have tested middle-aged adults; Jones may not have had a no-treatment control group. You may not mention this just to show off the fact that you noticed it. If your study contains middle-aged participants, then you can use Smith's results (emphasizing the missing middle-aged group) to provide a rationale for your own hypotheses or design.

Don't forget the rules on verb tense in your literature review. You are reporting on work that has been completed. Therefore, use past tense (found) or present perfect (have found). Even your own work has already been completed by the time you report the results. So use past tense when you talk about the purpose of your study, the hypotheses, or what the participants had to do. The exception to this is when your introduction concerns a research *proposal*. Students are often required to write introductions for this purpose, and in this case, the research is clearly not completed. For research proposals, use present and future tense in writing about your study (e.g., "the purpose is," and "the participants will").

▲ REMINDER BOX ▼

Use past tense to describe research findings—your own and those covered in your literature review.

The literature review may require the use of headings. The overall heading for the introduction is not used, but sometimes subheadings can be. When you just cannot think of a good transition sentence for your next paragraph, it may be time to consider breaking your review into sections. If you have a heading for a section, you can avoid that difficult transition sentence; the heading tells the reader where you are going. But don't abuse the help of headings. For example, don't use headings to avoid logical sequencing. Use them to enhance the evidence of your logic.

Here is where an outline will help you. Although everyone is taught that it is appropriate to outline a paper before writing it, some people just don't do it. You may find, however, that it is easier to outline your paper *after* you begin to write. Try an outline (if you have not used headings) when you finish your first draft. Be sure to print your draft first. This cannot be done from an on-screen manuscript. Outline the paper as it stands. If this proves difficult, you have not done a good job of organizing your paper. The topic sentences should guide you in your outline. If they are missing, this is the time for you to provide them. Outline again after your second draft. If you still cannot do it, ask someone else to try it, and if that person also finds it difficult to outline, ask why. A good literature review should be easy to outline.

▲ REMINDER BOX ▼

Try to outline your paper after it is written.

The *Publication Manual* is very explicit about how to organize your manuscript with headings. (Headings are especially useful in the Method section, and we will take them up again in Chapter 4.) A manuscript may have headings and subheadings. The subheadings may have subheadings of their own, and so on. These are referred to as *levels* of headings. Students' work is likely to have one, two, or three levels of headings. If you have one level, that means that none of your sections has a subsection. Your headings should be centered, and important words should begin with uppercase letters:

Here Is an Example of Such a Heading

If you have two levels, that means that your sections have subsections.

Your big units are headed as above, centered and containing upper- and lowercase letters. Your subheadings are also in upper- and lowercase letters, but they are up against the left margin and italicized. It looks like this:

Here Is the Main Heading

Here Is the Subheading

Here is the beginning of the paragraph you will write under this subheading.

Finally, if you have three levels, that is, if your subsections have subsections, it begins the same way. But your lowest level is indented with your paragraph, and only the first letter is uppercase. It ends with a period:

Here Is the Main Heading (Call it A)

Here Is the Subheading for That Section (Call it B)

    And here is the heading under that (call it C). This is the material that you will write under this section. When you are finished writing this material you can start a new section with a heading like C. When that is finished you may wish to do another, or else you can go back to the level above it—B. You are even allowed to have another big section start with the type of heading I've called A. However, follow the outline rules you already know: if you introduce a new level, be sure to have at least two subsections at that level. Believe it or not, the *Publication Manual* will take you through steps allowing you to use up to five levels. But don't try this at home.

A Few Additional Things to Think About When the Literature Review Is the Paper

It is not uncommon for students to prepare theoretical or practical literature reviews (or both). Of course, you will not want to include hypotheses or statements about your methodology if the review itself is the body of your paper. You can identify this type of article in a journal in one of several ways. First, you can notice that there is no Method or Results section. Second, the table of contents of the journal often breaks down the contents into sections. Look for articles that are not in the section called "Research." Finally, you can go straight to a journal that is devoted entirely to review articles, such as *Current Directions in Psychological Science* or *Psychological Bulletin.* These sorts of reviews can take several forms. You might find an article that is an attempt to provide the current state of the art on a topic—one that summarizes the most up-to-date and methodologically sound research on a topic. Some journals publish reviews that are more evaluative, reviewing the literature in order to make a case for a specific theory, and these could even be called theoretical articles. Also, there is a statistical method called meta-analysis that brings the findings of many different empirical studies together in one analysis. Articles of this type are also literature reviews, but with an emphasis on developing a statistical summary of the literature.

The opening sentence of the review resembles the opening sections you have studied. But the purpose will be different. The title may convey important information about the purpose of the review. The abstract often contains this information. In addition, you might find a statement of purpose in the concluding paragraphs of the article.

Exercise 10

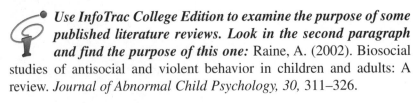

Use InfoTrac College Edition to examine the purpose of some published literature reviews. Look in the second paragraph and find the purpose of this one: Raine, A. (2002). Biosocial studies of antisocial and violent behavior in children and adults: A review. *Journal of Abnormal Child Psychology, 30,* 311–326.

1. _____

_____

Look in the first paragraph for the purpose of this one: Rivas, L. A. (2001). Controversial issues in the diagnosis of narcissistic personality disorder: A review of the literature. *Journal of Mental Health Counseling, 23,* 22–35.

2. _____

_____

For this meta-analysis, look in the first paragraph for the purpose: Orobio de Castro, B., Veerman, J. W., Koops, W., Bosc, J. D., & Monshouwer, H. J. (2002). Hostile attribution of intent and aggressive behavior: A meta-analysis. *Child Development, 73,* 916–934.

3. _____

_____

4. _____

_____

It is very difficult to organize a review paper because each topic presents idiosyncratic problems for the writer. In many ways it is easier to organize a paper based on your original research because the organizational structure is restricted by APA's own formula. Whether you are experienced with writing literature reviews or new to it, organizing the paper is always the most challenging part. But even though it seems as if each topic requires its own unique organization, it can still be instructive to see how others have handled this problem with their topics. If you scan a number of articles from *Current Directions in Psychological Science* or *Psychological Bulletin,* you will begin to see patterns that can help you.

Most reviews start with an introduction of their own of two to three paragraphs. This introduction, like that of the empirical research report, sets the context for the work: why this is an important issue, what sorts of people and how many have these problems or concerns, what are the public policy and/or practice issues that are affected by this problem. The thing to be careful of here, as noted before, is not to underestimate the expertise of your audience. Assume that they know that America is graying at a fast pace, that drugs are a problem in our high schools, and that in some settings therapists are burdened with a heavy caseload. Be very specific with your demographic information— restrict your context material to the narrow population that you are studying. And then get on with the show.

You wish to make a point with your review. You have an original contribution to make even if you have not done empirical research, because you have gained an original insight or perspective from your reading of the literature. That is why someone is going to rely on your work to gain a second-hand appreciation for what is out there. If you know where all this is going, you will have an easier time with the organization. Do not give in to the temptation to go through your material chronologically, unless you have decided that historical perspective is necessary for the reader to get your point. Usually, your point is that one way of looking at a psychological issue is the one you favor. That is an excellent start. How will you convince the reader? You will have to organize the studies in your review accordingly. But don't forget your obligation to present both sides of an issue fairly, noting which studies support each.

One good method is to organize around competing theoretical models (Bem, 1995). Some studies support one theory or model and some studies support another. Sometimes there are three or four models. If you think of your readings in these terms, then you will be likely to end by making a point about which model seems to be the most reasonable, given the evidence for it.

Many reviews end with suggestions for future research. But beware of ending with details for methodological improvements. Suggestions for further research as a final statement are best when they cover broad areas because the review itself covers a topic exhaustively, and the reviewer is in a position to see where large gaps in our knowledge may be. It can be interesting to end with something more memorable than suggestions for future research. This is a good place for bringing home your point of view in a more general way (Bem, 1995).

CHAPTER *4*

Preparing
the Method Section

The purpose of the Method section is twofold. First, by providing the details of the sample and procedures, you make it possible for other researchers to replicate your study exactly or to make explicit how they are deviating from your procedure. Second, after a reader knows the details of your method, it becomes possible to judge the reliability and validity of your experiment. Once you understand these joint purposes, you will be able to make decisions more easily about the level of detail you must achieve.

Organization

It is common for the Method section to be divided into subsections. These will generally include at least *Participants* (or *Subjects*) and *Procedure.* Often, the *Materials, Apparatus, Measures,* or *Stimuli* will be separated out from the Procedure and will constitute separate subsections. When archival data are used (data files that already exist—that is, you did not need to recruit participants to provide data), you may see *Sample* as a subheading instead of *Participants.* You are free to decide how subsections can best clarify your own work.

Exercise 1

Look at some research articles and copy the subheadings from the Methods section. Note that in editions of the *Publication Manual* prior to the fourth (1994) the word *subject* was used instead of *participant.* Therefore, in journals printed before this change went into effect, you will find a section called *Subjects* rather than *Participants.* In fact, some non-APA journals still accept the term *subjects.* You should use *participants* unless your group did not provide direct consent, as when you observe people engaged in some public activity.

 Find the answer using InfoTrac College Edition: Kuhn, D., & Udell, W. (2003). The development of argument skills. *Child Development, 74I,* 1245–1260.

1. Participants
   Materials
   Design and Procedure

2. Subjects
   Procedures
   Measures

3. _____

4. _____

5. _____

▲ REMINDER BOX ▼

The titles for the subsections of the Method section are flexible. Use them to your advantage.

Now let's consider the contents of some of these subsections.

Participants

Only the rules for human research subjects ("participants") will be considered at this time. Students more often report research with human subjects than with animal subjects, but be advised that the *Publication Manual* does explain how to describe animal subjects and I'll get to that later.

▲ REMINDER BOX ▼

People are participants; other animals are subjects.

Assuming, then, that you are describing human beings who provided data for an experiment, first indicate how many people participated. You must also provide some standard information about them and whatever information is relevant to your particular study. The most basic level of information about participants is age and sex. Report age ranges and means. Elsewhere in your manuscript standard deviations accompany all means, but this is not the convention for reporting the ages of participants. However, do indicate the appropriate unit of measure (e.g., years, months). If you have more than one group of participants, you do not have to report ages for each group unless the groups vary notably or intentionally. But you do have to indicate how many participants were in each group.

▲ REMINDER BOX ▼

Report age ranges and mean age of participants. Indicate the unit of measure.

Report how many men (or boys) and women (or girls) there were. The *Publication Manual* cautions against the use of the terms *male* and *female* as nouns. You should use *men* and *women* and *girls* and *boys* (high school age and younger) instead. You can use *males* and *females* if the age range includes both children and adults. Otherwise, use *male* and *female* only as adjectives (e.g., male experimenter, female clients, male and female adolescents). Do not use *elderly* as a noun; substitute *older adults* or *older persons.* Be careful also to used nonbiased labeling of sexual orientation. Preferred terms are *lesbians, gay men,* and *bisexual women* or *men.*

In the same spirit, do not reduce people to their diagnoses. It is better to say *people with bipolar disorder* than to call them *bipolars.*

▲ REMINDER BOX ▼

Use *men* and *women* instead of *males* and *females.*

Exercise 2

Copy sentences from the Participants or Subjects subsections of research articles that indicate the number, age, and sex of participants.

Find the answer using InfoTrac College Edition: Boisnier, A. D. (2003). Race and women's identity development: Distinguishing between feminism and womanism among Black and White women. *Sex Roles: A Journal of Research, 49,* 211–218.

1. One hundred women aged 35 to 55 (*M* age = 40.1 years) participated.

2. Participants were 32 undergraduates at the University of X (18 women and 14 men, mean age = 19.7 years).

3. The sample consisted of 17 male and 18 female research scientists and their spouses. They ranged in age from 40 to 65 years (*M* = 50.1).

4. _____

_____

5. _____

_____

6. _____

_____

Report general information about the nature of the population from which the participants come. For example, they may be students in psychology classes at a midwestern university or patients in a Boston hospital. Note how they were selected. Perhaps they volunteered, answered an advertisement, or were stopped on the street. Do *not* say that they were "randomly selected" unless they really were. That would mean that you had access to the whole population (of university students, patients at the hospital, or people on the street) and actually used a technique to select randomly (e.g., a coin toss, a table of random numbers, or numbers pulled out of a hat) the people you solicited to participate.

▲ REMINDER BOX ▼

Do not say "participants were randomly selected" when "participants volunteered" is more accurate.

Exercise 3

Copy sentences or phrases that indicate the general nature of the population of participants.

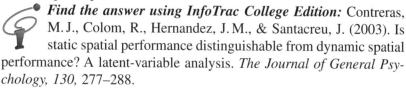

Find the answer using InfoTrac College Edition: Contreras, M. J., Colom, R., Hernandez, J. M., & Santacreu, J. (2003). Is static spatial performance distinguishable from dynamic spatial performance? A latent-variable analysis. *The Journal of General Psychology, 130,* 277–288.

1. One hundred women . . . living in rural communities in West Virginia agreed to participate.

2. The participants were 435 college students who completed an anonymous questionnaire and were paid $435.

3. All children were of middle to upper-middle socioeconomic status.

4. _____

5. _____

6. _____

Sometimes people are given something in return for their participation in experiments. Undergraduate psychology students may get extra credit or may participate as one way to fulfill course requirements. People may be paid money to participate. You must indicate what, if anything, was given to participants in exchange for their help with the experiment. Otherwise, you may just say they volunteered to participate.

If it is relevant to the study, you should specify the race or ethnicity of participants. The *Publication Manual* is specific with regard to which designations are preferred (e.g., *Asian* or *Asian American* rather than *Oriental; Native American* rather than *American Indian,* but in many cases the specific Indian group or nation would be best). Remember that racial and ethnic group labels are proper nouns and should be capitalized (e.g., *Black* and *White*). Always be sensitive to the changing standards for inoffensive labeling. A suggestion in the *Publication Manual* is that you ask your participants about their preferred designations if you are unsure. And remember that "hyphenated Americans" really have no hyphens in their spelling: Cuban American, African American, Asian American. This rule holds even if the labels are used together as a single modifier, for example, Irish American psychiatrists.

> ### ▲ REMINDER BOX ▼
> Racial and ethnic group labels are proper nouns. Capitalize them.

Often participants in research studies come from specific populations relevant to the nature of the study. They share some characteristic of interest. They may be children at certain grade levels, infants born full term, patients with specific diagnoses, people of specific sexual orientation, children whose parents are divorced, people with specific test score ranges, people above a certain educational level, people of a certain socioeconomic status, and so on. Some of the subfields of psychology operate with conventions of their own. For example, clinical research often contains diagnostic labels for participants; infant research may include minimum APGAR scores and/or minimum birth weights; educational level and/or verbal test scores may be included for older adult samples.

Exercise 4

Copy examples of specific descriptions of participants or of the criteria used to select them. As you do this, think about why these characteristics were noted by the researchers. (Thus, the characteristics noted for this exercise are more narrowly defined than for the previous one.)

 Find the answer using InfoTrac College Edition: Caron, A., & Ladouceur, R. (2003). Erroneous verbalizations and risk taking at video lotteries. *British Journal of Psychology, 94,* 189–195.

1. . . . who reported normal speech and hearing.

2. Participants were undergraduates who were not currently enrolled in a yoga class.

3. Participants were identical twins born less than 1 month premature.

4. _____

   _____

5. _____

   _____

6. _____

   _____

After you have made relevant information about participants clear to the reader, begin to use these more descriptive terms instead of referring to them as participants (e.g., the young and older adults, the children, the students, the physicians). Alternatively, you can use terms that describe the nature of their participation (e.g., respondents, perceivers, raters).

Sometimes participants are randomly assigned to groups, and at other times the grouping factor is based on some characteristic of the participants (e.g., age, sex, occupation, nationality, diagnosis). If the groupings are based on such characteristics, describe the details of this grouping in the Participants section. Do *not* say, "Participants were divided into men and women." Choose a phrase that indicates that you understand that you have no control over gender and that you merely grouped participants accordingly. If you randomly assigned participants to groups, it is usually more appropriate to indicate that you did so in your Procedure subsection.

Exercise 5

Copy sentences that indicate that participants were grouped according to subject characteristics.

 Find the answer using InfoTrac College Edition: Wenzel, A., Barth, T. C., & Holt, C. S. (2003). Thought suppression in spider-fearful and nonfearful individuals. *The Journal of General Psychology, 130,* 191–205.

1. There were 28 reading-disabled participants and 13 hearing-disabled participants.

2. The sample was composed of 100 meat packers who either (a) were still employed at the time of the experiment ($n=30$), (b) had resigned ($n=30$), or (c) had been fired ($n=40$).

3. _____

   _____

4. _____

   _____

5. _____

   _____

When participants are not randomly assigned to groups and are grouped instead by inherent characteristics, the groups may differ from each other in undesirable ways as well. For example, a divorced group may be older than a nondivorced group, or an older-adult group may have completed fewer years of school than a middle-aged group. When it is relevant to the research to demonstrate that these other variables have been controlled or that differences have been noted, a researcher includes a statistical analysis of these group differences in the Participants section. Thus, in this section you may find descriptive statistics and/or statistical comparisons of means of such variables as age, education, general health, or verbal ability.

▲ REMINDER BOX ▼

Statistics may be reported in the Participants subsection if they describe preexisting differences between groups.

When some participants do not complete the research tasks, it is necessary to indicate how many dropped out and why. Some percentage of infants get fussy; some adults do not come back for a second session (attrition); some people may not meet certain criteria after testing has begun. When surveys are mailed to participants, some are not returned. Indicate what percentage of surveys was actually completed. When participants do not complete the study, avoid saying that they *failed.* Say they *did not.*

Exercise 6

Copy sentences that refer to dropouts from experiments or survey return rates.

Find the answer using InfoTrac College Edition: Barrera, Jr., M., Glasgow, R. E., McKay, H. G., Boles, S. M., & Feil, E. G. (2002). Do Internet-based support interventions change perceptions of social support? An experimental trial of approaches for supporting diabetes self-management. *American Journal of Community Psychology, 30,* 637–654.

1. We excluded data from nine additional students because they had previously been in a bungee-jumping experiment.

2. Of the initial 300 participants, 45 did not appear for follow-up testing. Data from these participants are not included in any of the analyses.

3. _____

_____

4. _____

_____

5. _____

_____

The *Publication Manual* indicates that researchers are expected to treat participants in accordance with the ethical guidelines established by the APA. Sometimes a sentence to this effect appears toward the end of the Participants subsection. Your instructor may give you specific guidance about this if it is expected. The reason such a statement is often not included in a published article is that, for many journals, authors are required to attest to its truth in the cover letters they submit with their manuscripts. This requirement would appear in the instructions to authors printed somewhere in the journals. Thus, compliance with these guidelines can be assumed for all studies published in those journals, even though the articles do not attest to it in each case.

Apparatus

Include this subsection only if you have used special equipment. You must make clear what a research participant using this equipment actually *does*. It is often difficult for students to decide on an appropriate level of detail for a piece of equipment. There are two goals to keep in mind. The first is to allow readers to understand the experiment from the point of view of the participant. The second is to provide enough detail to allow replication of the experiment. When you describe the function of the equipment from the participant's point of view, concentrate on the task and the special nature of the equipment that facilitates it. For example, if you have a mirror tracing device, you need to mention that it is designed to allow someone to write with a pencil while looking only at the reflection of this action in a mirror. It is not appropriate to indicate how this looks from the experimenter's viewpoint or how difficult it is to set up.

> **▲ REMINDER BOX ▼**
> Describe devices from the point of view of the participant, not the experimenter.

If the device is available for purchase, provide the name of the company and the make and model number. If it is a computer, indicate what type. Computer programs may be described here if you are also describing anything about the computer itself or the keyboard. Otherwise, programs are often listed in the Materials subsection.

If you have constructed a piece of equipment, describe its function in detail. When you identify the parts of your apparatus, keep in mind that you must refer to these parts in a consistent way throughout your manuscript (e.g., the "red button" cannot later be called the "red key"). Remember that you must use metric units when giving details of size. You may use a diagram or a photograph if that would make it easier for the reader to understand. The *Publication Manual* directs that, if necessary, you may use an appendix to describe equipment you have constructed. As a general rule, when you have constructed a device, make clear in the text whatever is necessary for the reader to judge your work; include an appendix with additional detail only for those who wish to construct a similar device for purposes of replication. You do not need to describe ordinary furniture or its layout, stopwatches, or room dividers.

> **▲ REMINDER BOX ▼**
> Use metric units when describing the apparatus.

Exercise 7

List items you find in the Apparatus subsection of articles. Indicate whether the item was purchased, constructed, or a modified version of something purchased. You might have better luck with this exercise if you use journals describing infant research or research with nonhuman subjects.

 Find the answer using InfoTrac College Edition: Hund, A. M., & Plumert, J. M. (2002). Delay-induced bias in children's memory for location. *Child Development, 73,* 829–840.

1. Experimental chambers (constructed) . . .

2. Sessions were recorded by means of a Panasonic camcorder (purchased).

3. _____

_____

4. _____

_____

5. _____

_____

Materials

Materials in this sense usually refers to printed materials. These may also be called "stimuli." Audiotapes, videotapes, and computer programs sometimes are included as well. The same rules apply here as for the previous subsection: Allow readers to understand the task from the point of view of the participants while also providing enough information for replication. Likewise, in this subsection you may be using materials bought or borrowed (with appropriate citations) from other authors, or you may have constructed them yourself.

When you have used published tests or questionnaires, it is usually easy to list them in the Materials subsection. Give the author and year as you would any citation. Indicate what the test measures. Try to tie the terms to your Introduction section, in which you have noted how you operationalized your dependent measures (e.g., Jones and Smith's [1965] Warmth Test was used to measure empathy). If you have reliability and validity information that pertains to your population, include those references as well. Do not forget to give a brief description of the task or the items (you can provide sample items) from the point of view of the participant. State the meaning of the score (e.g., scores range from 15 to 45 with higher scores indicating higher levels of empathy). Use the past tense to describe what your participants did (e.g., the children placed a mark . . .) and the present tense to describe enduring characteristics of a test (e.g., the test measures . . . ; high scores indicate . . .).

Questionnaires and tests you devise yourself should be explained more fully. In addition to all of the information suggested for published tests, it is helpful to provide sample questions in the body of the paper and the complete test or questionnaire in the form of an appendix. Researchers often construct scales that require participants to choose a numerical response, for example, from 1 to 5. These may be referred to as Likert scales or Likert-type scales. The high and low points (1 and 5 in the current example) are called the *anchors* of the scale. There are two points of punctuation to learn about scales: there is a hyphen between the number and the word *point* (e.g., 5-point scale), and the anchors are italicized. Usually, the points between the anchors are not labeled, but if they are, these labels must also be noted and italicized.

▲ REMINDER BOX ▼

Italicize the anchors of a scale.

Exercise 8

Find examples of descriptions of scales. Copy sentences and phrases that indicate the number of points on the scale and the labels or anchors.

 Don't find the answer using InfoTrac College Edition— HTML does not reliably preserve italics from the original article.

1. Test A uses a 5-point Likert format with responses ranging from 1 (*almost never or never true*) to 5 (*almost always or always true*).

2. Participants indicated on a 5-point rating scale (1=*not at all true of me*, 5=*very true of me*).

3. Responses range from *not at all true of me* (1) to *totally true of me* (5).

4. _____

_____

5. _____

_____

6. _____

_____

Sometimes researchers use materials or stimuli that are not tests. They may be passages to read, lists to learn, videotapes to watch, diagrams to copy, and so on. As with tests, this type of material may have been developed by others and used as previously designed, developed by others and modified by you, or developed entirely for your experiment. Be sure to indicate the source accordingly. In describing these materials, follow the same rules of explaining the task from the point of view of the participant and giving enough detail for replication (perhaps in an appendix, table, or figure).

Exercise 9

Look for articles that have materials presented in appendixes. Find the sentence in the body of the article that refers the reader to the appendix. Copy that sentence and indicate briefly what kind of information about the material is presented in the body of the article.

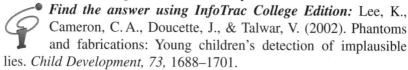 ***Find the answer using InfoTrac College Edition:*** Lee, K., Cameron, C. A., Doucette, J., & Talwar, V. (2002). Phantoms and fabrications: Young children's detection of implausible lies. *Child Development, 73,* 1688–1701.

1. A diagram is provided in the appendix.

2. In the appendix I discuss in detail . . .

3. A new scale was developed from existing measures and modified to be suitable for the current context. It is presented in the appendix.

4. _____

5. _____

6. _____

It is tricky to describe materials that vary by experimental condition before you have described the actual procedure. If the design and materials are interrelated (e.g., different word lists for different groups; vignettes whose protagonists vary by experimental group, etc.), remember that you are under no obligation to have a separate Materials subsection. You can use the label *Design and Materials* if this happens. In that subsection you explain that there were several groups, how participants were assigned to the groups, and what was (were) the independent variable(s) that controlled the grouping. Then the reader will be ready for the information that each group received slightly different materials. Some authors decide to include the description of materials within the

Procedure subsection or even after the Procedure subsection in order to solve this type of writing problem. Remember, a reader can become confused when there are several conditions that differ primarily according to the materials used, especially if you describe the materials before describing the conceptual differences among the conditions. Therefore, it may be better *not* to use a special Materials subsection than to confuse a reader with descriptions of sets of materials for various experimental groups before you have explained the purpose of the groups.

Procedure

The *Publication Manual* states that the purpose of this subsection is to "tell the reader *what* you did and *how* you did it" (p. 20). There are two points of view that you must be aware of in this part of the manuscript: the researcher's and the participant's. Use the researcher's point of view to describe how the experiment was organized, and use the participant's point of view to describe the task.

Start with the organization. What were the conditions? Did everyone participate in every condition (within-subjects design) or were people grouped in some way (between-groups design)? Were they grouped by some previously noted characteristic or randomly assigned? (Please remember that people are assigned to conditions; conditions are *not* assigned to people.)

Provide names for your groups or conditions that help the reader to remember the key distinguishing features. The *alcohol-information group* and the *no-information group* are better designations than Group A and Group B. Feel free to give a short name or abbreviation to a group after describing it. For example, the alcohol-information group might be the AI group, and the no-information group might be the NI group. Be sure to refer to the group consistently by that term in the rest of the manuscript. Note that the names of groups and conditions are not capitalized unless they have been given letter or number names (*Group A* but *alcohol-information group*). Usually, however, the abbreviations are written in all uppercase letters. Don't overdo abbreviations. If the reader is more confused than helped by a complex set of abbreviations, just use the entire words as labels.

▲ REMINDER BOX ▼

Capitalize the name of the condition only if the name is a letter or includes a number.

Exercise 10

Copy sentences from articles that include information about conditions or groups.

> *Find the answer using InfoTrac College Edition:* Popp, D., Donovan, R. A., Crawford, M., Marsh, K. L., & Peele, M. (2003). Gender, race, and speech style stereotypes. *Sex Roles: A Journal of Research, 130,* 317–325.

1. Half of the participants were randomly assigned to meet in face-to-face groups (FTF) and the other half watched videotapes (VT).

2. Participants were randomly assigned to one of the conditions of the 2 (letter: accurate vs. inaccurate) × 2 (hiring decision: favorable vs. unfavorable) factorial design.

3. Each participant saw one of the three taped sporting events.

4. _____

_____

5. _____

_____

6. _____

_____

Be careful with the terms *group* and *condition*. They are related and almost equivalent in the researcher's mind, but they are not linguistically equivalent. People can be in groups; they cannot be in conditions. Groups can perform tasks, but conditions cannot. It is often best to use participants as sentence subjects. For example, "Depending on condition, participants were told that they would hear A or see B."

▲ REMINDER BOX ▼

Use the term *condition* carefully. People are assigned to conditions, not the other way around. People can't be in conditions, and conditions can't perform tasks.

Once you have explained how the experiment was organized, explain the task. Start with the general nature of the task, and then give details that apply to all of the groups. Later, explain how the groups differed. Use the participant as the focus rather than the experimenter. That is, say the participants read, rated, completed, listened to, or watched. This is preferable to saying the experimenter gave the participant something to read, rate, complete, listen to, or watch.

Exercise 11

From Procedure subsections, copy examples of tasks that participants perform.

> *Find the answer using InfoTrac College Edition:* Holmes-Lonergan, H. A. (2003). Preschool children's collaborative problem-solving interactions: The role of gender, pair type, and task. *Sex Roles: A Journal of Research, 164,* 505–517.

1. Each participant was required to drink two beverages.

2. Participants were led to believe that a student was conducting a study of teacher ratings. They read that . . .

3. Participants labeled each photograph with the adjectives that seemed best to describe the person in that photograph.

4. _____

_____

5. _____

_____

6. _____

_____

Summarize instructions to participants. It is not usually necessary to provide verbatim instructions unless they are very unusual. However, if the experimental manipulation involves variations in the instructions, you should quote them exactly.

Explain the method of scoring only if it is not obvious. Thus, an answer of 3 on a 5-point scale will be understood to be scored as 3. But in a tracing task, you should mention whether an error was scored when the tracer's mark touched the pattern or went over the guideline. Was it another error when it came back in? If a summary score was calculated and used for data analysis, explain how that was done and refer back to the appropriate term in the hypotheses.

Finally, if your participants were deceived in any way, indicate that they were debriefed at some point in their participation.

Remember Your Audience

When in doubt about what level of detail to use, assume always that your audience is composed of experienced research psychologists.
They know:

1. *How to randomize:* Do not explain that you had one hat for men and one for women and that you put each condition label in each hat and pulled one out every time you got ready to test someone. Just say participants were randomly assigned to conditions or treatment groups. If additional details are relevant (e.g., with equal numbers of men and women in each group), state them briefly.

2. *The meaning of such terms as* counterbalance, control, *and* being blind to experimental conditions: Do not say that half of the group randomly got red first and then green, and the other half got green first and then red. Just say the order of presentation of the colors was counterbalanced.

3. *How to phrase instructions that stress speed and accuracy:* Do not say participants were told to read as fast as they could but to try not to make mistakes. Just say instructions stressed speed and accuracy.

4. *How to create an answer sheet for their own use:* Just say answers were recorded or responses were recorded verbatim.

5. *When to construct reminders for themselves:* Do not say the correct answers were written lightly in pencil on the backs of the cards so that the experimenter would know which answers were correct. Say nothing.

6. *How to handle ordinary materials:* Do not explain that participants used pencils to write on their answer sheets and that they gave them to the experimenter when they were finished. Just describe the answer sheets.

▲ REMINDER BOX ▼
Don't tell readers more than they need to know. Assume common sense and familiarity with experimental methodology.

A Few Words About Animals

When nonhuman animals are research subjects, the *Publication Manual* provides additional guidance. You must report the genus, species, and strain number or supplier and stock designation. Sex, weight, and physical condition are important. Indicate any special handling that affects replication efforts. As with humans, ethical treatment is assumed, because most APA journals will have their authors stipulate to that in their cover letters. Finally, use neuter pronouns: The rat waited in *its* cage (not *his* cage). Likewise, you will use *that* or *which* and refer to the rat *that* waited in its cage, not the rat *who* waited in its cage. The exception to this neuter gender rule is for those who name their animals, as primate researchers are wont to do. Once you have referred to your chimp as Elvis, you should later refer to *him* rather than *it*.

CHAPTER 5

Preparing the
Results Section

The Results section should contain the summary of the findings, including the results of statistical analyses. This section should be written in a form that is predictable. Report the statistical tests of your hypotheses in the order in which they were originally presented. Do not give in to the temptation to start with the finding you like best or end with one that supports your favorite hypothesis. Lead the reader through your analyses in the order that is most logical, not necessarily most exciting. Do not discuss which hypotheses were supported and which were not; those sentences belong in the Discussion section. This is not the place to concern yourself with variety of sentence construction. It is best to use the same sentence format for every result that involves the same type of statistic. The *Publication Manual* suggests that someone who has a copy of your data set should be able to reproduce your analyses if you have written your results well.

Results and Discussion can be combined into one section. This is often the case in published research when the two can be done relatively briefly. Many authors use this approach when reporting the results of more than one experiment in a single article. Each experiment contains a Results and Discussion section, and the article ends with a section entitled General Discussion. As a rule, students should have separate Results and Discussion sections unless directed otherwise by the instructor.

▲ **REMINDER BOX** ▼

State results in the order that corresponds to the order of the hypotheses as presented in the introduction.

Statistics

The *Publication Manual* is very specific about what kind of information to report for each analysis. For *t* tests, *F* tests, and chi-square tests, include the numerical value obtained for the statistic, degrees of freedom, and probability level. Reporting of confidence levels is also strongly recommended. For *F* tests, also include the mean square of the error term *(MSE)*. Indicate the direction of effect; for example, *Group A scored significantly higher than Group B* is better than *the scores of the two groups were significantly different.* Follow this information with the actual *t*-test result. You must report actual means and standard deviations (or some other measure of variability) whenever you report that means differed. These may be provided in a table.

▲ **REMINDER BOX** ▼

Whenever an effect is significant, report the direction of that effect.

Students are usually required to report a bit more information than is included in journals. For example, after a *t*-test result, you must indicate whether it was one-tailed or two-tailed. Also, you will have to include statistical values for all of your results, even the nonsignificant ones. Please note that the word *insignificant* does not belong in your paper. That is not a technical term; it is an insult. If you mean that the result was not significant you should use the word *nonsignificant.* No one will be insulted that way.

▲ **REMINDER BOX** ▼

Use *nonsignificant* rather than *insignificant* if an analysis does not yield an acceptable level of significance.

The *Publication Manual* advises that you report exact *p* values provided by statistical packages. The main thing to remember when reporting probability is to use the *less than* symbol and the *equals* symbol appropriately. If the value comes from a table, use the *less than* symbol (e.g., $p < .05$); if it comes from a statistical package, use the *equals* symbol (e.g., $p = .023$). But note this exception: If the computer printout indicates a probability level of .000, you should write $p < .001$. *P* values cannot be zero, so .000 on a printout indicates that the probability has been rounded off. The real probability may have been .0000071. If you drop the last zero in the value on your printout and replace it with a 1, and then claim that $p < .001$, you have made an accurate statement (.0000071 *is* less than .001).

There are only a few ways to phrase statistical reports. Collect some models now. Use only very recent journals for this exercise because the older journals may follow rules that are out of date.

Exercise 1

Copy sentences that contain *t*-test results. Note that *t* test is hyphenated when it is used as a compound adjective (as in *t*-test results), but not otherwise. Note also that statistical symbols are italicized.

 Find the answer using InfoTrac College Edition (first paragraph of Results section): Greitemeyer, T., Rudolph, U., & Weiner, B. (2003). Whom would you rather help: An acquaintance not responsible for her plight or a responsible sibling? *The Journal of Social Psychology, 143*, 331–340.

1. Overall mean ratings of freshness did not differ as a function of age, $t(49) = .03$, *ns* ($M = 6.12$ for old and $M = 6.50$ for new).

2. There was a tendency for managers to rate themselves as braver than did their employees, $t(50) = 12.37$, $p < .01$.

3. Independent sample one-tailed *t* tests showed that dogs scored significantly higher than cats on both the first test battery, $t(29) = 22.42$, $p = .021$, and on the second test battery, $t(29) = 19.32$, $p = .032$.

4. _____

_____

_____

5. _____

_____

_____

6. _____

_____

_____

Exercise 2

Copy sentences that contain chi-square results. Note that Greek letters are not italicized. Degrees of freedom and sample size are included in parentheses. Degrees of freedom are included for most other statistics as well, but sample sizes are not. You are also required to report cell frequencies, but these often appear on a table.

> *Don't find the answer using InfoTrac College Edition—Chi-square characters are not retained in HTML format.*

1. χ^2 difference between continuity on strong mutual versus strong unilateral affiliations $= 19.29$, $p < .001$.

2. There was a significant relationship, $\chi^2 (1, N = 31) = 10.4$, $p < .01$, between type of bird (chicken or turkey) and whether the gravy was with giblets or without.

3. _____

_____

4. _____

_____

5. _____

_____

Analysis of variance results usually contain the abbreviation ANOVA. The rule for abbreviations is the same for the Results section as for the rest of the manuscript. Introduce the abbreviation in parentheses the first time you use the term, and then use only the abbreviation thereafter. If you do not use the term a second time in the manuscript, do not introduce the abbreviation at all. The abstract does not count as part of the manuscript for this rule.

▲ **REMINDER BOX** ▼

Introduce abbreviations in parentheses and use the abbreviations rather than the full term thereafter.

Usually the *F* test is reported for the ANOVA. Students have varying degrees of familiarity with ANOVA results. Undergraduates are likely to have experience with one-way analyses and analyses using two independent variables. Therefore, these will be the focus here.

If you compared three or more means in a one-way analysis, report the results using the term *one-way analysis of variance.* Remember that a significant finding means at least one mean was different. Because this lacks precision, authors usually do planned or post hoc tests on these means. Planned comparisons are reported as such. Post hoc tests are usually named (e.g., Tukey or Scheffe) and a significance level is targeted prior to the calculation. You are also expected to provide cell means, cell standard deviations, and an estimate of the pooled within-cell variance. These often appear on a table.

Exercise 3

Copy sentences from Results sections that report one-way ANOVAs. If planned comparisons or post hoc tests were done, include those sentences.

Find the answer using InfoTrac College Edition (for a one-way ANOVA with post hoc comparisons, go to the last paragraph of the Results section): Elbedour, S., Bart, W.M., & Hektner, J. (2003). Intelligence and family marital structure: The case of adolescents from monogamous and polygamous families among Bedouin Arabs in Israel. *The Journal of Social Psychology, 143,* 95–110.

1. We analyzed mood judgments using a one-way ANOVA. Participants in the elated condition rated themselves most elated, followed by participants in the neutral condition and those in the positively grim condition, $F(2,100) = 21.35$, $MSE = 7.95$, $p = .004$. See Table 1 for means and standard deviations.

2. _____

_____

_____

3. _____

_____

_____

4. _____

_____

_____

Analyses with two independent variables require the reporting of main effects and interactions. The safest way to report these is either with both main effects preceding the interaction, or with the interaction first. Do not report one main effect, the interaction, and then the other main effect. Again, as with *t* tests, if you say a main effect was significant (e.g., "The main effect of color was significant"), take the opportunity to say right at that time what the direction of the effect was (e.g., "The main effect of color was significant, with the blue-pencil group scoring higher than the green, *F* . . .").

Interactions generally leave you two choices for phrasing: (a) "The interaction between age and instructional condition was significant, *F* . . ." or (b) "The Age × Instructional Condition interaction was significant, *F*. . . ." Capitalization rules are somewhat unexpected: main effects are lowercase, but interactions are capitalized.

Do not be concerned that you have several sentences in a row that are the same in structure. The reader will not be put off by this but rather will appreciate the clarity.

▲ REMINDER BOX ▼
Capitalize interaction terms but not main effects.

Exercise 4

Find sentences that report 2×2 ANOVA results. Copy what you find, including main effects and interactions.

Find the answer using InfoTrac College Edition (look in third paragraph of Results section): Howe, N., Rinaldi, C. M., Jennings, M., & Petrakos, H. (2002). "No! The lambs can stay out because they got cozies": Constructive and destructive sibling conflict, pretend play, and social understanding. *Child Development, 73,* 1460–1473.

1. We examined mean cooking times for experimental and control ovens using a 2 (gender) $\times$ 2 (condition) analysis of variance (ANOVA). Overall, men cooked more slowly than women, $F(1, 62) = 60.51$, $MSE = 27.74$, $p < .0001$. Cooking was on average 1.1 s slower in the control oven, $F(1, 62) = 40.32$, $MSE = 16.21$, $p < .05$. The Gender $\times$ Condition interaction was significant, $F(1, 62) = 29.11$, $MSE = 2.20$, $p < .01$.

2. Cooking times were subjected to a 2×4 mixed ANOVA . . .

3. An analysis of variance performed on these data yielded the following results: group, $F(1, 50) = 18.10$, $MSE = 3.21$, $p < .05$; oven type, $F(1, 50) = 21.44$, $MSE = 32.81$, $p < .01$. The Group $\times$ Oven Type interaction was not significant.

4. _____

_____

_____

5. _____

_____

_____

6. _____

_____

_____

Correlation results require the correlation coefficient, r, and the p value. Reporting correlation results can be a preposition nightmare. These are acceptable statements of correlation:

X correlated significantly with Y

X and Y were significantly correlated

The correlation between X and Y was significant

The correlation of X and Y was significant

Correlations among X, Y, and Z were computed

The correlation of X with Y was significant

Exercise 5

Copy sentences that contain correlation results.

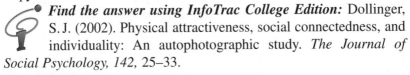 ***Find the answer using InfoTrac College Edition:*** Dollinger, S. J. (2002). Physical attractiveness, social connectedness, and individuality: An autophotographic study. *The Journal of Social Psychology, 142,* 25–33.

1. The correlation between swimming speed and hiking speed was not significant, $r = -.17$.

2. The correlation between age and facial expressivity was unreliable $(r = .06)$, whereas the correlation between shoe size and facial expressivity was significant $(r = .51, p = .003)$.

3. _____

_____

4. _____

_____

5. _____

_____

You must report means and standard deviations, but you do have some choice about where. They may be presented in a table, in the text, or in parentheses right after the statistic that compared them.

> ### ▲ REMINDER BOX ▼
> When statistical analyses are used to compare means, provide all relevant means and standard deviations in the text or in a table, but not in both.

The *Publication Manual* strongly advises authors to report effect size estimates as well as significance tests. A few authors routinely report η^2 (eta squared) with *F*-test results: $F(1, 115) = 623.16$, $MSE = .01$, $p < .01$, $\eta^2 = .83$. There are a variety of effect size estimates to choose from, and your instructor will guide you.

Exercise 6

Copy a sentence that contains effect size results.

 Find the answer using InfoTrac College Edition: Koch, C. (2003). Preconceptions of taste based on color. *The Journal of Psychology, 137,* 233–242.

1. We calculated the effect size of video recording of interviews (versus the audiotaped baseline) using eta squared as the estimate of effect size, $\eta^2 = .63$.

2. The effect size (η^2) was .76.

3. _____

    _____

Likewise, authors are encouraged to report power estimates, particularly when they wish to discuss results that do not achieve statistical significance.

Exercise 7

Look for an example of power analysis.

 Find the answer using InfoTrac College Edition (look toward the end of the Participants subsection): Slaughter, V., & McConnell, D. (2003). Emergence of joint attention: Relationships between gaze following, social referencing, imitation, and naming in infancy. *Journal of Genetic Psychology, 164,* 54–71.

1. The . . . was not significant, $F(2, 201) = 0.03$, $p > .05$; the power to detect this effect at alpha = .01 was greater than .95.

2. _____

_____

3. _____

_____

Tables and Graphs

The *Publication Manual* advises that tables should be used sparingly because they are inconvenient for readers and expensive to publish. Your professor may instruct you to present certain findings in tabular fashion to give you practice. If the decision is up to you, use the suggestion in the *Publication Manual* that a table with only three numbers probably presents data that could more conveniently be provided in the text. The APA guidelines are unique and complex for tables. Although some basic rules are presented here, if you prepare a table, consult the *Publication Manual* for further directions. Another good source is Nicol and Pexman's (1999) *Presenting Your Findings,* a book published by the APA that can guide you in formatting tables. Tables should be numbered with arabic numerals in the order that they are mentioned in the text. In addition, tables have titles that give an indication of which variables are contained in them but without duplicating all of the words labeling rows and columns. For example, *Mean Happiness Ratings for All Conditions* is better than *Mean Happiness Ratings and Standard Deviations for Fun Condition, Pain Condition, and Basketball Condition.* Locate the table number in the upper left corner of the page and place the title, italicized, below it.

Next, consider the words identifying the rows and columns. Every column needs a heading, even the one on the far left that probably contains words (e.g., independent variables) rather than numbers. Often column headings are organized into several layers. Organize this with a view to presenting items next to each other that the reader wants to compare. For example, all means should be next to one another. A means table may be organized like this:

Table 1

Means for Age Groups as a Function of Instructional Condition

	Mean Score			Standard Deviation			Sample Size		
Age Group	Verbal	Written	Control	Verbal	Written	Control	Verbal	Written	Control

Align columns carefully with plenty of space between columns. Note that APA-style tables have horizontal lines separating each row of headers, but they have no vertical lines separating columns. Tables also end with a line spanning the last row of data. Under that line you will find additional notes explaining abbreviations or symbols and also footnotes relating to *p* values. Everything in the table is double-spaced, even the lines spanning the columns. Many types of tables (e.g., means tables, correlation tables, ANOVA tables) have a basic format, and you should look for models in journals that contain the type of data you wish to present. Nicol and Pexman (1999) also provide many models for these and other tables. You may find that my example of the organization of means and conditions is inverted in comparison to samples that you find. Mine is based on newer guidelines in the fifth edition of the *Publication Manual.*

Contrary to what you might expect, tables are placed at the end of your manuscript, *after* the References section.

Exercise 8

Find two tables that display data you understand. Copy the titles of the tables and the headers.

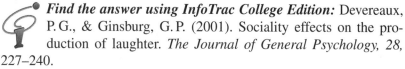 ***Find the answer using InfoTrac College Edition:*** Devereaux, P. G., & Ginsburg, G. P. (2001). Sociality effects on the production of laughter. *The Journal of General Psychology, 28,* 227–240.

1. Title: _____

_____

Column headers: _____

_____

2. Title: _____

_____

Column headers: _____

_____

If you do use a table, you must refer the reader to it by number and indicate what will be found there. This is a good time to think about verbs and sentence subjects again. If a table is to be the grammatical subject of a sentence, just what can it do? Do tables *contain* numbers? Do they *display* them? Perhaps. Alternatively, the contents of the table may be the grammatical subject, and then you must figure out what relationship the contents have to the table. Are numbers *on* a table? *In* a table?

Exercise 9

Find out now just what acts tables can legally perform. Copy sentences from Results sections that refer readers to tables.

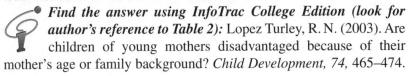 ***Find the answer using InfoTrac College Edition (look for author's reference to Table 2):*** Lopez Turley, R. N. (2003). Are children of young mothers disadvantaged because of their mother's age or family background? *Child Development, 74,* 465–474.

1. Table 3 presents correlations . . .

2. Table 3 indicates frequencies . . .

3. Table 4 summarizes the results of the regression analysis.

4. Mean scores appear in Table 4.

5. _____

6. _____

7. _____

Tables are good for presenting data when you want to be precise. There are a lot of means tables in print because people often like to see exact means when means are being compared. Correlation tables are an efficient way to show many correlations at once; correlation graphs are not. Graphs are better for illustrating patterns in your results. They are often used to present statistical interactions. If you are presenting more than 20 data points, the *Publication Manual* advises you to use a graph. For examples of how to present a variety of graphs, see *Displaying Your Findings: A Practical Guide for Creating Figures, Posters, and Presentations,* by Nicol and Pexman (2003).

Be aware that all illustrations other than tables are called Figures, and their titles appear on a page of their own, entitled Figure Captions. All figure captions (but not table titles) appear on this page, which comes before the figures themselves. All of this is found *after* any tables you have included.

Line graphs and bar graphs are very common in psychology journals. It is best to produce your graphs with a graphics program that allows a degree of customization. That way you'll be able to follow a lot of very specific APA guidelines, a few of which are presented here. The independent variable is plotted on the x axis and the dependent variable on the y axis. The y axis should be shorter than the x axis (the y axis is often about two-thirds the length of the x axis). Choose a scale that includes all the data without a lot of empty space. The axes must be labeled and the unit of measure must be included in the label.

For a line graph, differentiate lines by differentiating plot points. Use clear open and solid circles and triangles as plot points. Lines should all be solid rather than dashed or dotted. For a bar graph, use simple shading techniques to distinguish between sets of bars. White (no shading) and black are preferable to grays and stripes. If you need a third shade, use diagonal stripes. Do not use color for graphs.

Place a legend inside the graph area. Do not label the lines themselves in a line graph; explain the meanings of the shapes of the plot points or the shadings of the bars in the legend. As with tables, figures are numbered consecutively in the order in which they are referred to in the body of the manuscript. Write the figure number lightly with a pencil (e.g., Figure 1) on the top right front of the page containing each graph, and write the word *top* on the back of the page to show which way is up. Also write the manuscript page header on the back. There is no title except on the figure caption page.

Exercise 10

Find some graphs that make sense to you. Copy their titles.

Find the answer using InfoTrac College Edition: Rikers, R., Winkel, W. T., Loyens, S., & Schmidt, H. (2003). Clinical case processing by medical experts and subexperts. *The Journal of Psychology, 137,* 213–224.

1. _____

2. _____

3. _____

When referring the reader to the graph of your results, you face the problem of subject and verb again. What can a figure legally do? What relationship do the contents of the figure bear to the figure itself?

Exercise 11

Copy sentences from Results sections that refer readers to figures.

Find the answer using InfoTrac College Edition: Vaughn, S., Linan-Thompson, S., & Hickman, P. (2003). Response to instruction as a means of identifying students with reading/learning disabilities. *Exceptional Children, 69,* 391–409.

1. Inspection of Figure 3 indicates . . .

2. As can be seen in Figure 2, . . .

3. Figure 1 illustrates . . .

4. _____

5. _____

6. _____

▲ REMINDER BOX ▼
Refer to all tables and figures at least once in the body of the paper.

Even if you have decided to list means and standard deviations in the text as a way to avoid the difficulties of creating tables and figures, you are not off the hook yet. You face the decisions of where to put them and how to refer to them. You can put them after the statistic that indicates that they are significantly different from each other. If there are two means, use the word *respectively* to indicate order: "Mean scores for meat eaters and vegetarians were 6.10 ($SD = 0.43$) and 5.12 ($SD = 0.23$), respectively." Do not forget standard deviations. You can also squeeze this information into the sentence that reports a *t*-test result by using parentheses. You should use abbreviations for mean (*M*) and standard deviation (*SD*) when they are in parentheses: "Meat eaters (*M* = 6.10, *SD* = 0.43) scored significantly higher than vegetarians (*M* = 5.12, *SD* = 0.23), *t* . . ." Always indicate what the mean refers to (e.g., mean ratings, mean scores, mean number correct).

Exercise 12

Copy sentences from Results sections that contain information about means and standard deviations.

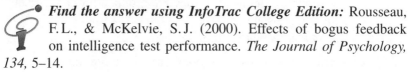 ***Find the answer using InfoTrac College Edition:*** Rousseau, F. L., & McKelvie, S. J. (2000). Effects of bogus feedback on intelligence test performance. *The Journal of Psychology, 134,* 5–14.

1. A post hoc test showed that race car drivers (*M* = 100.00, *SD* = 10.13) and go-cart drivers (*M* = 101.30, *SD* = 8.45) drove at significantly higher speeds than did bus drivers (*M* = 48.15, *SD* = 7.02).

2. Women had, on average, longer fingernails than men (women: *M* = 8.35 cm, *SD* = 0.83, men: *M* = 6.42 cm, *SD* = 0.65).

3. _____

   _____

4. _____

   _____

5. _____

   _____

Useful Rules

1. Letter symbols (e.g., *N, p*) are italicized.

2. Greek letters are *not* underlined or italicized.

3. Letters that are abbreviations (e.g., *M, SD*) should be used only in parentheses. In the narrative, use the word (e.g., mean, standard deviation).

4. Use the symbol for percent (%) whenever it is preceded by a numeral (e.g., 3%).

5. Use spaces between symbols and within equations as if each term were a word (e.g., $p < .05$).

6. Use numerals for 10 and above, words for nine and below.

   Exceptions:
   a. Never begin a sentence with a numeral. Look up spellings for numbers in the dictionary and pay attention to hyphen use.
   b. Use numerals below 10 if they are grouped for comparison with numerals above 10 (e.g., 3 out of 14 trials).
   c. Use numerals below 10 in an abstract.

7. Use metric units unless the nonmetric is more familiar (e.g., 3×5 cards). In this case put the metric equivalent in parentheses.

8. Use a zero before a decimal point when the value of a number is less than 1, unless it can never be more than 1 (e.g., levels of significance, proportions, correlation coefficients).

9. Rounding off: Use two decimal places when reporting inferential statistics and, in general, *p* values. For means, use two decimal places as long as relevant differences can be seen with two decimal places. Otherwise try to rescale, for example, converting centimeters to millimeters.

10. Abbreviations for any measurement you are likely to need are listed in the *Publication Manual.* Note that most, but not all, abbreviations for units of measurement are neither capitalized nor followed by a period. Leave a space between the numeral and the abbreviated unit of measurement.

11. The plural of *analysis* is *analyses.*

12. *Between* is used for two things: Correlations *between* two variables. *Among* is used for three or more: Correlations were computed *among* three variables.

13. Word your sentences so that statistical results are not in parentheses. Many statistical results contain parentheses of their own (containing degrees of freedom, for example). Set off these statistical results with commas instead.

14. Do not use mathematical symbols as if they were verbs in your sentences. For example, the following is *incorrect:* The number of boys = 17. You can use the word *equals* if you really must write a

sentence that uses it. The word *was* is also nice here. Use the symbol for mathematical terms when those terms are inside parentheses.

15. Common fractions are expressed in words (e.g., one half of the sample, three fourths of the liquid) and others are expressed as numerals (e.g., 31.2 pastries).

CHAPTER 6

Preparing the
Discussion Section

The *Discussion* section contains three types of material. The first can be called *inevitable.* It is inevitable that the results will be evaluated in terms of the research questions and/or hypotheses generated in the introduction. Each statistical analysis was done in an effort to answer one of these questions or test one of these hypotheses. The results of these analyses have been reported in the Results section. In the Discussion section, you must, inevitably, indicate which analyses lead to what answers, or which analyses support or do not support which hypotheses. When hypotheses are supported, you will then, inevitably, refer to the theory or theories that generated those hypotheses. When hypotheses are not supported, you will inevitably admit it and look back to the method for enlightenment. It should be clear that the inevitable part could be written by anyone who really understood the introduction and results.

The second type of material found in the Discussion section is *creative,* and the creative part can only be written by you. This type of creativity is the type that characterizes the creative researcher, not the poet. You need to step back mentally from your findings and think about what else might be interesting about them. If hypotheses are supported, are there other explanations that a creative thinker might come up with besides the happy thought that your hypotheses are simply perfect? In the case of hypotheses that were not supported, what possible explanations exist? Would it be reasonable to make a minor adjustment in a hypothesis in the light of a given result, or are there confounds in the method? Here we are not talking about technical problems that result from undergraduate foul-ups, but rather real methodological issues that might interfere with the results of the most sophisticated laboratory crew. If your results are entirely unexpected (perhaps significant but in the wrong direction) you can bring in literature you have not mentioned in the introduction to place these unexpected findings in a new context. Most of the literature you refer to in the inevitable part of the discussion should have been mentioned in the introduction, but there are exceptions in this creative part.

The third part is *confessional.** This refers to the limitations of your study. You must admit that this is not the ultimate answer to the pressing problem you defined in your introduction. You must explain what cautions are necessary in interpreting this finding.

The *Publication Manual* provides less guidance for the format of the Discussion section than students would like. And because it is more creative and freewheeling than the other sections, it is difficult for students to know when they have written enough. They sometimes resort to noting trivial shortcomings (e.g., not enough participants) and overbroad applications (e.g., this study should help teachers of students with learning disabilities). However, it is possible to overlay a format of three unofficial sections on most fairly short Discussions. I will call them first part, second part, and third part so that you can conceptualize them. But remember that these demarcations are used here as guideposts—they are *not* to be used as subheadings in your actual Discussion section.

First Part—Inevitable

The Discussion should begin with an assessment of the results of your main hypothesis. Usually, the entire hypothesis is restated in a sentence concerning its support or nonsupport. It is appropriate to remind yourself at this point that your experiment was designed to test a hypothesis, not a theory. A theory probably led to the hypothesis, and support of many such hypotheses lends support to the theory, but you must first deal with the hypotheses in your discussion. Students sometimes forget that experiments do not *prove* or *confirm* hypotheses. The best way to

---

*I am indebted to Margaret Gatz for suggesting this term.

convert the inferential statistics in your results into plain English for the discussion is with the word *support* or the phrase *fail to support.*

▲ **REMINDER BOX** ▼

Start your discussion by referring to the main hypothesis. Indicate which statistical result appears to support it or fails to support it.

Exercise 1

Select several Discussion sections and look at the first sentence or two of each. Copy examples of opening passages that state whether or not the main hypothesis was supported. When several hypotheses have been tested and several statistics have been reported, you may find that the author indicates which specific result or analysis is tied to a specific hypothesis. However, the Discussion section is not a place to restate the results, but rather to explain and interpret them.

Find the answer using InfoTrac College Edition: Kebbell, M. R., Johnson, S. D., Froyland, I., & Ainsworth, M. (2002). The influence of belief that a car crashed on witnesses' estimates of civilian and police car speed. *The Journal of Psychology, 136,* 597–607.

1. As expected, participants provided with salty foods requested more water than did those provided with unsalted foods.

2. The experiment reported here provides strong support for the general contention that the sun rises in the east.

3. The present findings fail to support the hypothesis that exterminators reliably detect termite infestations better than do third graders.

4. _____

   _____

5. _____

   _____

6. _____

   _____

Recall that some studies are designed not to test hypotheses that imply direction of effect but rather to answer questions, describe characteristics, assess relationships, and so on. When this is the case, the word *hypothesis* will be missing from the first sentence of the discussion, but there will be some reference to the purpose of the experiment as it relates to the statistical analyses.

Exercise 2

Copy the first sentence or two of Discussion sections that refer to major results in terms of research questions or purposes other than hypothesis testing. *Hint:* Check first for introduction sections that end with research questions rather than hypotheses. Then copy the first sentence of those discussions.

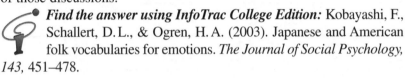 ***Find the answer using InfoTrac College Edition:*** Kobayashi, F., Schallert, D. L., & Ogren, H. A. (2003). Japanese and American folk vocabularies for emotions. *The Journal of Social Psychology, 143,* 451–478.

1. The central findings of the experiment are that . . .

2. The results of Experiment 1 showed that . . .

3. _____

   _____

4. _____

   _____

5. _____

   _____

Second Part—Creative

After the general statement that refers back to the hypotheses or purposes in the introduction, you may find it difficult to classify all of the types of comments that follow. The *Publication Manual* is brief in its explanation of the contents of the discussion, and authors have more leeway in this section than in the others. Try to find just a few examples of each of the kinds of comments that can be included in this section.

Exercise 3

Look for statements of similarity between this work and that of previous researchers or other works by the same author.

Find the answer using InfoTrac College Edition: Mohr, P. B., & Larsen, K. (1998). Ingroup favoritism in umpiring decisions in Australian football. *The Journal of Social Psychology, 138,* 495–504.

1. Our results support Ripley's belief that the truth is stranger than fiction.

2. Consistent with previous research, this study revealed that . . .

3. _____

4. _____

5. _____

Exercise 4

Look for statements that show differences between this work and that of previous researchers or other works by the same author.

Find the answer using InfoTrac College Edition: Mulcare, S. L., & Aguinis, H. (1999). Effects of adoptive status on evaluations of children. *The Journal of Social Psychology, 139,* 159–172.

1. Given the data from our experiments, it is clear that liberty is not preferable to death, as Patrick Henry proposed.

2. Unlike previous studies, ours showed that graduate student trainees are indeed able to control their outbursts.

3. _____

_____

4. _____

_____

5. _____

_____

Exercise 5

Look for comments that refer to theories or theoretical contexts referred to in the introduction.

Find the answer using InfoTrac College Edition: Updegraff, K. A., McHale, S. M., & Crouter, A. C. (2000). Adolescents' sex-typed friendship experiences: Does having a sister versus a brother matter? *Child Development, 71,* 1597–1610.

1. These findings suggest a limit to the use of the theory of relativity in explaining the motion of the planets.

2. Consistent with a mediation model, this study showed that . . .

3. _____

_____

4. _____

_____

5. _____

_____

Exercise 6

Look for acknowledgment of alternative explanations for the findings—explanations other than the "truth" of the hypotheses or theories that appear to be supported.

Find the answer using InfoTrac College Edition: Benenson, J. F., & Christakos, A. (2003). The greater fragility of females' versus males' closest same-sex friendships. *Child Development, 74,* 1123–1129.

1. Another possible cause for the higher death rates among the younger skydivers in this study could be their refusal to use parachutes.

2. One explanation for this inconsistency is . . .

3. _____

_____

4. _____

_____

5. _____

_____

You must acknowledge negative results. What can you do with results that fail to support your hypothesis? In the light of these results, you might reconsider the theory. What would be the ramifications of adopting a weaker version of the theory, or, more extreme, of abandoning the theory? Perhaps your failure to extend a previous finding sheds light on the population to which it can reasonably be extended.

Exercise 7

Copy a few references to and explanations of negative results.

Find the answer using InfoTrac College Edition: Montague, M., & van Garderen, D. (2003). A cross-sectional study of mathematics achievement, estimation skills, and academic self-perception in students of varying ability. *Journal of Learning Disabilities, 36,* 437–449.

1. The test did not reliably distinguish first-year college students from third-year students in their ability to spell correctly. It is possible that, contrary to our hypothesis, college attendance does not develop this skill. Alternatively, it may be that some majors are more likely to attract good spellers than others.

2. _____

_____

_____

3. _____

_____

_____

Remember to discuss *all* of your results. If you just did one statistical analysis, you are ready to go on to the third part. If you tested more than one hypothesis or question, you will return to the first part and cycle through the second part again before going on. Begin the next section after you have discussed all of your results individually.

▲ **REMINDER BOX** ▼

Be sure to discuss the results of each of the analyses reported in the Results section.

The *Publication Manual* instructs that you discuss the implications of the work. *Implications* are the logical consequences and the larger significance of the outcome. If hypotheses are supported, implications are inevitable and should flow directly from a well-written introduction. The logical consequence of a supported hypothesis is a supported theory. This is in itself the larger significance of the outcome. The introduction will have made plain why this is valuable information. Restate some of these reasons. If hypotheses are not supported, you must think creatively and speculate about practical and theoretical implications. Try to end the discussion with a paragraph that makes it plain why psychologists, even those from other specializations, should find your work important.

Exercise 8

Find some words and phrases in Discussion sections that signal implications.

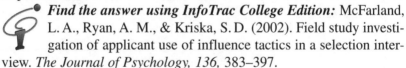 *Find the answer using InfoTrac College Edition:* McFarland, L. A., Ryan, A. M., & Kriska, S. D. (2002). Field study investigation of applicant use of influence tactics in a selection interview. *The Journal of Psychology, 136,* 383–397.

1. The present findings open a new window to the investigation of . . .

2. . . . makes a contribution to an accumulating literature . . .

3. If clinicians want their clients to develop to their maximum potential, they might consider [doing what I did with the experimental group].

4. _____

5. _____

6. _____

7. _____

A specific type of implication can point to a practical application. For example, the significance of the work is that it provides guidelines for how people in certain situations should act or should be treated. But not all research has immediate practical applications. Some research is "pure" and will only lead to applications after much intervening research. If nothing practical comes to mind, don't force the point.

▲ REMINDER BOX ▼

A relatively easy and concrete item for discussion for the new researcher is the practical application of the finding. Do this if it seems reasonable for the type of study under discussion.

Exercise 9

List examples of how practical applications are mentioned in Discussion sections.

 Find the answer using InfoTrac College Edition: Morrow, P. C., & Leedle, T. (2002). A comparison of job performance and disciplinary records of smokers and nonsmokers. *The Journal of Psychology, 136,* 339–349.

1. Researchers and clinicians should be careful about . . .

2. . . . recommend that memory improvement programs should emphasize . . .

3. _____

4. _____

5. _____

The last part of a Discussion section often contains suggestions for future research. Remember that this kind of suggestion must come directly from the discussion that precedes it. Sometimes students, feeling the need to suggest some future research, suggest something completely arbitrary. Be careful about this. For example, following a discussion of results related to a reaction time test of color naming, it is not appropriate to suggest that future research be done on color-blind people or people who speak other languages. A sure sign that you are falling into the trap of suggesting irrelevant future research is a sentence that begins, "It would be interesting to see if . . ." Suggest future research only if you can suggest what the next *logical* research question would be. Don't forget the verb lessons you learned in studying the Introduction section: If "future research" is to be the grammatical subject of the sentence, your verb choices are limited.

Exercise 10

Copy phrases that indicate how suggestions for future research are tied to the rest of the Discussion.

 Find the answer using InfoTrac College Edition: Lin, S. (2000). Coping and adaptation in families of children with cerebral palsy. *Exceptional Children, 66,* 201–218.

1. Future research should focus on identifying the magnitude of the individual parts of the bigger thing whose magnitude I just identified.

2. Continued exploration of the relationship between the two variables [I studied] is necessary to determine which of the competing explanations for [what I found] accounts for how this happens outside the lab.

3. A study is needed that traces [this thing I found] by comparing two groups over time.

4. _____

_____

_____

5. _____

_____

_____

Third Part—Confessional

There should be a discussion of weaknesses in the study. This should not be a big part of any Discussion section, however. After all, if the experiment were truly weak, you would not have undertaken it. It is far more likely that you will discuss "limitations" rather than "weaknesses." You should imagine yourself trying to outfox potential critics of your study and acknowledge these shortcomings yourself. This has the effect of making the reader feel intelligent for having noticed something before you even mentioned it, rather than feel argumentative about your conclusions.

Are the results generalizable to only a portion of the people to which this hypothesis is supposed to apply? Of course. Indicate exactly what the limits of generalizability are. It is always possible to question the degree to which laboratory results generalize outside of the lab, but is there anything about yours that points especially strongly in that direction? Have you used correlational results to indicate the possibility of causality? Now is the time to remind the reader that this type of conclusion must be made with caution. Is it possible that someone else might have operationalized a construct in a different way than you did? Admit it. However, feel free to defend your decisions in the same paragraph.

▲ REMINDER BOX ▼

You are obligated to note the limitations of your study, but do leave out the trivial ones and the ones that might apply to any study ever undertaken.

Exercise 11

Look through Discussion sections for indications of the limitations of experiments. List the types of limitations that you find.

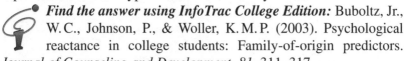 *Find the answer using InfoTrac College Edition:* Buboltz, Jr., W. C., Johnson, P., & Woller, K. M. P. (2003). Psychological reactance in college students: Family-of-origin predictors. *Journal of Counseling and Development, 81,* 311–317.

1. The cross-sectional design does not give direct evidence of change in the variable of interest.

2. The findings are not generalizable to some other group.

3. The self-report method provides only an indication of how people actually behave in . . .

4. _____

5. _____

6. _____

Exercise 12

List specific words and phrases that are used to present limitations.

Find the answer using InfoTrac College Edition (Look at the fourth paragraph of the Discussion section): Truchot, D., Maure, G., & Patte, S. (2003). Do attributions change over time when the actor's behavior is hedonically relevant to the perceiver? *The Journal of Social Psychology, 143,* 202–208.

1. One limitation of the study is . . .

2. It could be argued that . . .

3. One concern is that . . .

4. At least two caveats should be mentioned . . .

5. _____

6. _____

7. _____

Sometimes the confessional section is the last part of the discussion. It is better, however, to slip it in before the implications. That way you end with a brag instead of an apology.

Verb Tense

Remember the conceptual difference between past and present tense as it relates to a discussion of your research. Your experiment is over; your results have been analyzed. Reference to what you and your participants did and what you found is always in the past. Statements about human behavior in general are in the present. The implications of your study should be discussed in the present tense. As a result of these directives, your Discussion section is likely to be primarily in the present tense: results *support* the hypothesis; limitations of the study *are;* findings *contribute* to the literature; the results *suggest;* they *support* the findings of other researchers; performance on these measures *involves.*

▲ REMINDER BOX ▼

Use past tense to describe your results and present tense for statements about human behavior in general.

Exercise 13

List subject–verb phrases found in the present tense in Discussion sections.

Find the answer using InfoTrac College Edition: McCutcheon, L. E., Ashe, D. D., Houran, J., & Maltby, J. (2003). A cognitive profile of individuals who tend to worship celebrities. *The Journal of Psychology, 137,* 309–322.

1. One explanation that may account for the results is that . . .

2. When both parents are present, teenagers may feel inhibited.

3. Although these experiments demonstrate that the sky is blue, additional questions await further research.

4. _____

5. _____

6. _____

Exercise 14

List subject–verb phrases found in the past tense in Discussion sections.

Find the answer using InfoTrac College Edition: Leach, D. J., Wall, T. D., & Jackson, P. R. (2003). The effect of empowerment on job knowledge: An empirical test involving operators of complex technology. *Journal of Occupational and Organizational Psychology, 76,* 27–52.

1. The results of Experiment 3 showed that . . .

2. The present study examined . . .

3. It is unlikely that our results were due to bad weather.

4. _____

5. _____

6. _____

CHAPTER **7**

Preparing the Abstract

The abstract is the part the reader approaches first, but it is the part the writer approaches last. By the time you are ready to write your first abstract, you will already have read and "used" abstracts for at least some of the purposes for which they are intended. And understanding what readers need from an abstract is the best way to begin learning how to fulfill these needs in your abstract.

Here are some of the types of readers you will be addressing:

1. *Someone who needs an overview of an article he or she is definitely about to read.* This reader might be a student doing required reading, an expert determined to keep up with everything written in a certain narrow field, or someone who was so attracted by the title that nothing will stop the process. This type of reader needs an outline that will facilitate cognitive processing of the article. Technical writing is not dependent on surprise endings, and technical reading is aided when outcomes are known in advance.

2. *Someone who is browsing through a journal looking for something interesting to read.* This reader might be someone who subscribes to the journal (probably an expert) or someone passing time in a library (perhaps an expert in a related field or a student). This reader

appreciates the fact that all abstracts follow a similar format so that quick comparisons can be made on content. This person wants to know how a certain article will advance his or her professional knowledge—will it be relevant because of its theoretical context, methodology, or outcomes?

3. *Someone who is searching an abstract-retrieval system (such as PsycInfo).* This reader might be a student looking for sources for a paper, a professor looking for relevant readings to assign, an author deciding which journals are most likely to publish articles like the one he or she is preparing, a researcher looking for data on a measure he or she is about to use, a graduate school applicant looking for all of the articles written by the faculty of a program he or she is considering. Sometimes the outcome of these searches is a list of articles the searcher intends to look at or read. At other times, it is a fact-checking mission and begins and ends with abstracts only. Sometimes, it is a fishing expedition, and the searcher may or may not decide to look at entire articles.

How can all of these types of readers be served by the same 120-word summary? There are two parts to the answer. First, the contents are narrowly specified in the *Publication Manual.* Therefore, readers will always be able to predict that they will find certain types of facts in every abstract. Second, the style is designed so that it can stand alone and still be very informative.

▲ REMINDER BOX ▼
An abstract contains 100 to 120 words.

Contents

The abstract of a research report should contain key facts from each section of the report. Try using about one sentence each with information from the Introduction, Results, and Discussion sections and up to two sentences from the Method section. This general rule should keep you within the required 100 to 120 words while allowing for each of the types of information specified in the *Publication Manual.*

From the introduction, extract the key element from the portion devoted to the purpose of the study and reduce it as much as you can. This information is usually contained in the first sentence of the abstract.

Exercise 1

Find the first sentence of abstracts that begin with a global statement of purpose. Copy those sentence frames.

> **Find the answer using InfoTrac College Edition:** Bowker, A., Gadbois, S., & Cornock, B. (2003). Sports participation and self-esteem: Variations as a function of gender and gender role orientation. *Sex Roles: A Journal of Research, 49,* 47–58.

1. Aims were to determine _____ and identify related variables.

2. The effectiveness of _____ on the _____ functioning and mental health of _____ was examined.

3. To determine whether _____ and _____ with and without _____ complaints differ in the nature of the activities they do in _____ circumstances, the authors developed and evaluated the _____ scale.

4. _____

   _____

   _____

5. _____

   _____

   _____

   You must state facts about the participants that are particularly relevant to the study. Include at least number, age, and gender. If participants are not human, include genus and species.

Exercise 2

Copy statements from abstracts that provide facts about subjects or participants.

> *Find the answer using InfoTrac College Edition:* Sadeh, A., Gruber, R., & Raviv, A. (2003). The effects of sleep restriction and extension on school-age children: What a difference an hour makes. *Child Development, 74,* 444–455.

1. Fifty men and 52 women from a suburban population (age 26–64) . . .

2. The study included 100 women and their mothers who were living in multigenerational households that included a child under age 5.

3. _____

   _____

4. _____

   _____

5. _____

   _____

State the major elements of the method, including the apparatus, test names, and/or procedures. If a well-known test is the main element you need to mention, it may be included in the same sentence as the participant description. Alternatively, if the method is unusual, you may need to use two sentences.

Exercise 3

Copy statements from abstracts that provide facts about methods.

Find the answer using InfoTrac College Edition: Urani, M. A., Miller, S. A., Johnson, J. E., & Petzelk, T. P. (2003). Homesickness in socially anxious first year college students. *College Student Journal, 37,* 392–399.

1. Participants viewed pictures of insects and described their wing shapes.

2. . . . watched televised doctors and lawyers who endorsed various laundry products.

3. _____

4. _____

5. _____

State the major findings. Do this in English, not in statistics, but do include significance levels. You will not have space for secondary findings. Indicate only those that refer to the major purpose expressed in the abstract.

Exercise 4

Copy statements of research findings from abstracts.

 Find the answer using InfoTrac College Edition:
Niedzwienska, A. (2003). Gender differences in vivid memories. *Sex Roles: A Journal of Research, 49,* 321–331.

1. The percentage of tree trimmers with low, medium, and high trimming speed scores who retired before age 55 was 79.3, 50.1, and 49.2, respectively.

2. _____

   _____

3. _____

   _____

Finally, the abstract contains a statement (of the type found in the Discussion) concerning the conclusions, implications, and/or applications of the study. Choose from the following types of statements: what was demonstrated, what the consequences are of what was demonstrated, or in what way the study should be appreciated and by whom.

Exercise 5

Look at the final sentences of some abstracts. Copy statements or sentence frames that seem to summarize the major points of the Discussion sections.

 Find the answer using InfoTrac College Edition:
Armstrong, K. H., Dedrick, R. F., & Greenbaum, P. E. (2003). Factors associated with community adjustment of young adults with serious emotional disturbance: A longitudinal analysis. *Journal of Emotional and Behavioral Disorders, 11,* 66–77.

1. In addition to the better known _____, the [measure used in this study] is an important predictor of . . .

2. For [one type of participant] depression was predicted by [certain variables] and for [the other type] it was predicted by [other variables].

3. Findings extended prior research by demonstrating that . . .

4. _____

_____

5. _____

_____

6. _____

_____

Style

The best way to write your own abstract is to follow the preceding guidelines without concern for length in your first draft. When you have done that, you will probably find that you have gone over the 120-word limit. Before attending to some of the stylistic elements that will help shorten your abstract, go over it to make sure that it is accurate and self-contained. This editing session may even increase the length of your abstract, but consider why it is so important. Many people, as described earlier, will never read your entire article. For their sake your abstract must be able to stand alone and to report reliably what is in the paper.

▲ REMINDER BOX ▼

An abstract is accurate and self-contained. Some people will never read the rest of the article.

So reread your abstract, making sure that you have not included new information and that you have included the major purpose, result, and contribution of your study. If you have extended or replicated someone else's work, reference to that work must also be in the abstract (authors' initials and surnames and year of publication). That way, someone following up the work of a certain author will find yours in a keyword search. However, there is no references list associated with the abstract. The full reference information for studies referred to in your abstract will be at the end of your paper in the regular references section.

▲ **REMINDER BOX** ▼

Include the major purpose, result, and contribution of your study in the abstract.

The *Publication Manual* specifies that the third person is preferable to the first person in an abstract. It also says that verbs are preferable to their noun equivalents and that active voice is better than passive. Therefore, reread with an eye to how your sentences can be strengthened accordingly. For example, do not write "Participants were asked for their opinions about . . ." Change to more active language: "Participants rated . . ."

▲ **REMINDER BOX** ▼

Use active rather than passive voice in the abstract.

Now reread again, making sure this time that the abstract can stand alone. Do not use unusual abbreviations. Define terms that may not be known to a psychologist with a different specialty. If you have given your treatment groups nicknames or abbreviations, do not use them in the abstract (unless you will refer to them twice in the abstract—then present abbreviations in parentheses the first time, as you would in the paper itself).

▲ **REMINDER BOX** ▼

Do not use unusual abbreviations in the abstract.

After you are sure you will not need to add anything else to your abstract, and assuming you are over the 120-word limit, it is time to see what characters, words, or phrases you can delete. First apply the rules that are specific to abstracts: Use numerals instead of words for numbers under 10, unless they begin a sentence; use abbreviations in the text that would normally be allowed only in parentheses (like *etc.* or *vs.*); use abbreviations that are commonly understood by psychologists even if you are using the terms only once (e.g., ANOVA and WAIS-R).

▲ REMINDER BOX ▼

Use common abbreviations in the abstract without using whole words to introduce them.

Next look for phrases that are not dense with information and try to omit them. For example, omit "the results revealed that" and "the conclusions are that." Omit phrases that repeat information provided by the title of the paper.

See if sentences can be combined to save words. For example, perhaps you can include participant and procedure information in one sentence: "Undergraduate students (25 men and 25 women) rated 5 types of odors." You might be able to combine purpose and results by reordering and combining: "The hypothesis that _____ was supported in an experiment that assessed _____."

Do not be discouraged if you are still over the limit. Writing an abstract is a very difficult task. Deleting words and phrases that have been written with great effort is an emotional and intellectual strain. Consider trading abstracts with a partner if you still cannot find a place to delete words. It is often easier to slash phrases from someone else's work than from one's own.

When you finally determine that your abstract fulfills all of the criteria discussed so far, you have only one task left. Imagine all of the people who might search an abstract-retrieval database and be glad to find your abstract. What key words would these people be likely to use in their search? Make sure that all of those words are actually in your abstract so that all of these potential searchers will find your work.

▲ REMINDER BOX ▼

Include all the words that someone doing a keyword search would be likely to need.

In typing your abstract, note that it should be a single, nonindented paragraph. The word *Abstract* is centered at the top of the page, just like other section headings.

CHAPTER 8

Preparing the
References Section

Students often notice that APA style has a *References* section instead of a *Bibliography.* The difference is important. In your References section, you list the works you have referred to in your paper. A bibliography is usually more extensive than a references list and may contain material you read but did not cite. Your references list should be in one-to-one correspondence with the sources you have mentioned in your paper. It should be accurate; readers may wish to consult some of your sources for their own edification. It should not contain anything you did not actually have in front of your eyes; secondary sources should be listed when appropriate, rather than primary sources you did not read.

▲ REMINDER BOX ▼

Include in the references section only those sources that you cited in your paper and only those you actually consulted.

If you read only one chapter of a book, you must list only that chapter. Usually, this occurs in the case of an edited book with chapters by various authors. Sometimes, however, you will consult part of a book written by a single author. In this case, the *Publication Manual* provides specific formats for indicating which chapter and/or pages you consulted.

There are so many types of material that may be consulted that it is not necessary to familiarize yourself with all of them until you need them. In this chapter, you will learn about the three most common types of references that occur in student papers: journal articles, chapters in edited books, and authored books (the same person[s] wrote the whole book). If you have used any of the others, consult the *Publication Manual* for details.

Word Processing Hints

- The references section begins on a new page, but it has a heading whose level is equivalent to the other major sections (e.g., Results), so it is typed, centered, at the top of the page. The rest of the manuscript (with the exception of the Abstract) is continuous; that is, no other section begins at the top of a page unless it happens to fall that way.

- Double-space everything on these pages, both within and between references on the list. Each entry should begin with a *hanging indent.* That means the first word is at the left margin and all other lines for that reference are indented 1.2 inches.

- Never type authors' first or middle names. Use only their initials and leave a space between initials.

Journal Article Reference

Author(s). (Year). Article title. *Journal Title, volume number,* page numbers.

Here are the rules:

1. Authors, last name followed by initial(s).
   - Use the ampersand (&) before the last author.
   - Place a comma between author names.
   - Place the comma before the ampersand, even if there are only two authors in the list.

2. Year of publication.
   - Place it in parentheses.
   - Follow with a period.

3. Title of the article.
   - ■ Capitalize only the first word in the title and the first word after a colon (even if these are only little words like *the*), when applicable.
   - ■ Follow this with a period.

4. Title of the journal.
   - ■ Capitalize each important word.
   - ■ Italicize the title of the journal.
   - ■ Follow this with a comma.

5. Volume number of the journal.
   - ■ Italicize it.
   - ■ Follow it with another comma.

6. Issue number.
   - ■ Almost never include this. Do so only if each issue of the year starts with page 1. Usually, scholarly journals begin each *year* with page 1, and each *issue* begins with the page that follows the last one in the previous issue.
   - ■ If you should have to include this, place it in parentheses after the volume number.
   - ■ Do not italicize it.

7. Page numbers.
   - ■ Include the full range (e.g., use 125–127 rather than 125–7 or 125–27).
   - ■ Do not italicize the page numbers.
   - ■ Finish up with a period.

   Journal article examples:

   - ■ One author:
     Rogers, M. (1989). My sweater has a zipper. *Children's Television Review, 12,* 120–122.

   - ■ With two authors, use an ampersand and comma between them:
     Rogers, M., & Kermit, F. (1994). Not all sweaters have zippers. *Children's Television Review, 14,* 12–30.

   - ■ With three authors:
     Rogers, M., McDonald, R., & Kermit, F. (2002). Not all creatures wear sweaters. *Children's Television Review, 17,* 124–130.

   - ■ With more than six authors, name the first six, then et al.:
     Rogers, M., McDonald, R., Kermit, F., Bird, B., Mouse, M., Brown, C., et al. (1984). And so on . . .

Exercise 1

Using InfoTrac College Edition, find a journal article and cite the reference as it would appear on a reference list.

_____

_____

Chapter in an Edited Book

Chapter author(s). (Year). Chapter title. In Book Author(s) (Ed[s].), *Book title* **(page numbers of chapter). Place of publication: Publishing company.**

Here are the rules:

1. Chapter author(s)' last name(s) followed by initials.
   - ■ Same rules as for journal article.

2. Year of publication.
   - ■ Same rules as for journal article.

3. Title of the chapter.
   - ■ Same rules as for journal article.

4. The word *In.*

5. Editor(s)' name(s).
   - ■ Initial(s) then last name—not last name first.
   - ■ Separated by commas and ampersand as for authors, but no comma for only two authors.

6. (Ed.) or (Eds.).
   - ■ Follow with a comma.

7. Title of the book.
   - ■ Italicize it.
   - ■ Capitalize only the first word in the title and the first word after a colon, when applicable.

8. Page numbers of chapter.
   - ■ Use the form pp. xx–xx.
   - ■ In parentheses.
   - ■ Follow with a period.

9. Place of publication.
   - ■ City and state or city and country—unless it is well known. If so, use city only.

- Use postal abbreviations for state.
- Follow with a colon.

10. Publishing company.
   - End with a period.

   Chapter in an edited book example:

   Smith, T. J., & Jones, R. N. (1971). Very interesting stuff: Relationship between grades and dental cavities. In J. Lennon & P. McCartney (Eds.), *A big book of interesting stuff* (pp. 22–125). London: British Publishing Co.

Exercise 2

Copy one listing from a References section for a chapter in an edited book.

 Don't use InfoTrac College Edition—HTML does not preserve the correct format.

_____

_____

An Authored Book

Author(s). (year). *Title.* **City: Publisher.**

This is a book written entirely by the same author(s), rather than with chapters contributed by various people.

   Authored book example:

   Smart, I. M. (1995). *Fun with psychology.* Green Hill, IL: Green Publishing Co.

Exercise 3

Copy a listing for an authored book.

 Don't use InfoTrac College Edition—HTML does not preserve the correct format.

_____

_____

Electronic References

As with the material described previously, this section will not be an exhaustive guide to these formats. Consult the *Publication Manual* or the following Web site for formats not covered here: http://www.apastyle.org/elecref.html You can check spelling for words like *online* and *Internet* here: http://www.apastyle.org/spelling.html.

When you want to cite an entire Web site, as I just did, do what I just did: give the address in the text and put no entry in the references list.

But if there is a document you want to cite, notice that you can find all or most of the same elements you need for print documents. Include the author and date in the text and list the full citation on the references page. After you have included all of the information specified for journal articles, indicate what date you retrieved it from the Web and the Web site. Here is an example for a journal article retrieved from the Web:

> Simpson, B. (1999). Cartooning and counseling. *Journal of Multimedia Psychology, 2*, 220–227. Retrieved March 5, 2001 from the World Wide Web: http://www.apa.org/journals/simpson.html

(You can insert a line break after a slash, but do not use a hyphen.)

It is possible that the document you retrieve is not a journal article, but rather an item written by someone just for posting at the Web site. If that is the case, treat it more like a book when you list it. Here is an example:

> Simpson, B. (1999). *Cartooning and psychology.* Hollywood, CA: American Psychological Association. Retrieved March 5, 2001 from the World Wide Web: http://www.apa.org/journals/simpson.html

Be careful with final punctuation. Putting a period at the end of a sentence or reference entry that would come after the URL address can cause an error for someone searching for that site. If there is no period in the address itself, leave it off the sentence, too. (See the last sentence in the first paragraph of this section.)

Capitalization rules for URLs are as follows: Everything up to and including the host name (www.apa.org in the preceding example) is in lowercase. The rest must match exactly what you found on the Web.

Exercise 4

Go to http://www.apa.org and search for a document you like. Cite it here:

_____

_____

Alphabetizing

Alphabetize according to the last name of the author who is listed first in each source. Keep the following in mind:

- Do not rearrange the order of authorship of any given article or chapter. If the article lists the authors as Smith, R. T., & Jones, A. L., do not list them as Jones, A. L., & Smith, R. T.

- Works by the same author are listed by year of publication, with the earliest first.

- If you have the same author listed first with different coauthors for different articles, arrange them alphabetically within the listing for that author, according to the second author of each entry. List Smith, R. T., & Jones, A. L. before Smith, R. T., & Marks, B. J.

- If an author appears as a single author of one source and the first coauthor of another, list the single-author source first and then the one with the coauthor (following the principle that "nothing" goes before "something"). List Smith, R. T. before Smith, R. T., & Jones, A. L.

Exercise 5

From a list of references, copy two listings by the same author for works published in different years.

 Don't use InfoTrac College Edition—HTML does not preserve the correct format.

_____

_____

_____

Copy two listings in which publications by two or more authors are headed by the same author.

_____

_____

_____

_____

References in the Body of the Manuscript

In the text, your citation would look like either of these: "Smith and Jones (1991) found . . ." or "The findings on altruism (Smith & Jones, 1991) . . ."

As noted in Chapter 2, the latter is usually preferred. The authors' names are typically not relevant to the point you are making, and if they are not directly relevant, then they are parenthetical.

When you are quoting from a source, use double quotation marks. Single quotation marks are only used when the author you are quoting is quoting someone else. In that case, the source contains double quotation marks, and these become single quotation marks in your manuscript. Final punctuation goes inside the quotation marks. When your quotation contains 40 or more words, use block form. That means that instead of using quotation marks, place the entire quotation in indented form. Indent one-half inch from the left margin (in line with the start of paragraphs) and keep every line of the quotation indented just the same amount. Do not change the right margin; use the same right margin as in the rest of your manuscript.

You will have to cite the page number of the source for direct quotations.

Do so after the closing quotation mark and before the period:

Freud (1950) reported "Blah blah blah" (p. 23).

If you want Freud's name in parentheses, do it like this:

"Blah blah blah" (Freud, 1950, p. 23).

When this occurs after a block quote, it comes after the final punctuation:

Mary had a little lamb whose fleece was white as snow. Everywhere that Mary went the lamb was sure to go. He followed her to school one day which was against the rule. The teacher was surprised to see a lamb at school. (p. 23)

Please recall the rule you read in Chapter 2: long quotations and frequent short quotations do not belong in a psychology paper.

Page references for online sources can be challenging; they are not paginated. If paragraphs are numbered, use that number (e.g., para. 3). If they are not, use headings as locators (e.g., Explicit Communication section).

Here are some final quirks for referencing in the body of your paper:

- Use the ampersand in parentheses and the word *and* in the text.

- Use commas only for three or more authors.

- When the work has two authors, always use both names (Michael & Jordan, 1987). When it has more than two and fewer than six authors, name them all the first time you cite them (Reebok, Nike, Keds, & Converse, 1988). In future references, name only the first and use *et al.* instead of the rest of the names on the list (Reebok et al., 1988). When the work has six or more authors, use *et al.* after the first author's name even the first time you cite them.

- If you are referring to more than one article inside the same parentheses, use a semicolon to separate the references. List them in the same order as they would appear in the References section. Here is an example: This hypothesis has received robust support (Ames, 1991; Roberts & Emerson, 1993; Simmons et al., 1990).

CHAPTER 9

Preparing a Title Page and Formatting Your Manuscript

Many people write with a working title in their minds but find that the finished product is actually an imperfect match for the original title. Students working on laboratory assignments generally work from the title of the lab as listed in the syllabus, but that is often an inappropriate title for the actual research report. Therefore, it is common for both professionals and students to compose the final title after the manuscript is written.

Like any title page, the title page of your APA-style manuscript contains the title of your paper, your name, and other identifying data. In addition, it contains information unique to APA style that is intended for the convenience of the editor and printer of the journal to which the article may be submitted: the manuscript page header and the running head. The difficulties students have involve (a) composing a good title and (b) understanding the difference between the manuscript page header and the running head.

Writing a Title

The *Publication Manual* directs that titles

1. Be 10 to 12 words in length
2. Make sense standing alone
3. Name the important variables or theoretical issues
4. Identify the relationships among variables

It is no wonder that students need practice in writing titles that conform to all of these requirements. Often after accounting for variables and being sure to make sense, authors find themselves with very long first-try titles. That is nevertheless a good way to begin.

Write everything you think you need without worrying about length. At this point it helps to think of the problem as a word puzzle, and very often word puzzles can be fun. First, get rid of anything unnecessary, such as "A Study of" or "An Investigation of." The title, "An Investigation of the Relationship Between Hat Size and Performance in Undergraduate Research Methods Classes," would benefit from that kind of cleanup.

Now you might find yourself with a title that starts with the words "The Effect of" or "The Relationship Between." This is not the best way to start. First, it is likely that you can save words if you find another way to convey this idea. Second, it is wise to begin with a word of specific importance to your study because when researchers glance through a list of titles in order to decide what to read, their attention is captured best by the first word. Choose your first word or phrase so that it applies uniquely to your own study. After all, every title of an experimental study could begin with "The Effect of." "Hat Size Effects on Performance in an Undergraduate Research Methods Class" conveys this uniqueness in the first words.

▲ REMINDER BOX ▼

Create titles that begin with important variables.

Exercise 1

It is worthwhile to look at some creative approaches to this "effect of" problem and work backward. Copy some titles that start with keywords.

1. "Gender Influences on Face Recognition Errors." This works better than "Effect of Gender on Face Recognition."

2. "Manners and Monkeys: The Effect of Social Reinforcement in Teaching Primates to Use Forks." Sometimes authors put a catchy phrase up front, and follow with "effect of."

3. "Do Mice Dream? The Relationship Between Rapid Eye Movements and Smiling in Sleeping Mice." Sometimes authors start with the research question and then move on to the variables.

4. _____

5. _____

6. _____

In scanning titles for Exercise 1, you have undoubtedly noticed many that began with "The Effect of." You have also seen some alternatives, and three probably stand out: the question title, the colon title, and the "and" title. The question title ("Do Mice Dream?") works because it is attention grabbing. The colon title works because it allows important variables ("Manners and Monkeys") to be named before the word *effect* or *relationship* is used, but these words can still be used for clarity. The "and" title names the variables, uses *and* between them, and requires that the reader infer which is the dependent and which is the independent variable. If you use an "and" title, be sure that there is little likelihood that a reader could make the wrong inference. ("Monkeys and Manners" is just as informative as "Manners and Monkeys.")

The Parts of the Title Page

Now that your title is written, you have only to follow some rules about getting it on a title page.

1. Type the title centered horizontally and in the upper half of the page. Capitalize each word, not the whole title. Do not use a font different from what is in the body of the paper and do not use bold type. If you use two lines because your title cannot fit on one line, double-space between them and break the title at a meaningful point, not whenever the line is full. "Gender Influences on the" is not a good first line for a two-line title.

2. Center your name one double space below the title. Decide today what your professional name will be. Most people use a first name and middle initial. But some people have names that are more complex than others, with two middle names or a hyphenated last name. Decide how it should look, but do not stray far from the first

name–middle initial–last name approach. You may change your name between your first publication and your last, but you should not change your professional name if you want people to know who you are. Again, use uppercase and lowercase letters, nothing fancy. Do not use the word *by*.

3. Center the name of your institution one double space below your name.

4. Your instructor may want additional information such as course number and date. If you have no specific instructions, just stop with name and institutional affiliation.

5. Create a manuscript page header. Use the header command on your word processor to create a flush right header that starts with the title page. The header contains the first two or three words of the title (even if they make no sense by themselves) followed by five spaces and then a page number. The reason for putting the beginning of the title in the header is that pages might be separated during the review and printing phases of journal work. Something handy must be used to identify which page goes with which manuscript (another good reason to avoid "effect of" titles). Your name is not appropriate because journal editors decide what to publish after articles are reviewed by people "blind" to the name of the author.

6. Decide on a running head of 50 characters (letters, spaces, and punctuation all count). The running head is a short version of your title that *does* make sense. If your title itself contains fewer than 50 characters, just use the title. The running head is what would be used as the page header in the actual printed journal and what helps readers find their place or remember what they are reading. This running head is placed on your title page flush left near the top and is identified as the running head. Type the words *Running head* followed by a colon. Then type your running head in all uppercase letters. Here is an example:

Running head: TABLE MANNERS FOR PRIMATES

▲ REMINDER BOX ▼

Pay attention to the difference between the manuscript header and the running head. The manuscript header is on the top right of every page, contains the first two or three words of the title (often does not make sense) and the page number. The running head of 50 characters or less makes sense and summarizes the title. It appears only on the title page, on the upper left.

Exercise 2

Copy some running heads (look in the upper margins of journal articles) and the titles of the articles to which they refer.

You need a journal here; you can't find running heads in InfoTrac College Edition.

1. _____

   _____

2. _____

   _____

3. _____

   _____

Formatting

By the time you are preparing your title page, you are probably just about finished with your paper. Read instructions in the *Publication Manual* about typing your manuscript. Here are a few things students sometimes forget:

1. The manuscript header should appear on the title page and every other page except those containing figures. For figures, hand write the header on the back.

2. The running head appears only on the title page.

3. Start a new page after the abstract and for the references. Do not start any other sections with a new page.

4. Double-space everything. There are no exceptions.

5. Use a 12-point font that is easy to read and looks like standard printing or typing. Courier and Times New Roman are good choices.

6. Use at least a 1-inch margin on all sides. Your word processor's default setting should work fine for this.

7. Do not allow your word processor to right-justify your lines. The right margin should be "ragged." You may have to fiddle with your software's default settings to accomplish this. Look for an "alignment"

command and choose "left." That way you'll get a straight left margin and a rough one on the right.

8. Do not allow your word processor to hyphenate at the ends of lines. This will probably also mean fiddling with default settings. Try finding "line and page breaks" somewhere in the paragraph or document formatting menu. Any hyphen that appears at the end of the line should be a "hard hyphen": one that belongs there, whether it is the end of a line or not.

9. Use your spell-checker wisely. It can help you spell words correctly if the word you have typed does not exist. It will not help you if you type *there* instead of *their*. Use your spell-checker, and then use your brain.

▲ REMINDER BOX ▼

Do not begin the Method, Results, or Discussion section on a new page. Double-space throughout. The right margin should not be justified. Do not hyphenate at the ends of lines except in the case where a hyphen is required as part of the spelling of that word.

CHAPTER 10

Grooming Tips
for Psychology Papers

You would probably never think of getting ready to go to class without checking your hair. If you eat onions before class, you probably grab a breath mint. You would never leave the table without making sure there is no food on your face. You don't want people to think you are careless with your appearance, and you certainly don't want them to think you are messy or smelly. You want to make a good impression. In the same vein, why would anyone think that a good impression could be made by turning in papers with careless mistakes, messy grammar, and punctuation that offends?

Some people have a flair for prescriptive rules of grammar and punctuation. They seem to be born knowing how to avoid run-on sentences. Others need to spend time learning these things, and some of these people get to college with a few gaps in their understanding.

This chapter contains a review of some rules of punctuation and grammar to which most college students have already been exposed. I have selected only a few rules because a psychology class is not the place to learn everything there is to know about grammar and punctuation. I have selected these particular ones because psychology papers seem to call for them quite often, and, in my experience, psychology professors complain that many papers they grade contain errors based on the failure to apply these rules.

For each of these rules, I have provided at least one example of proper usage in psychology journals. Find others.

Parallel Construction

Whenever elements of a sentence have the same function, their form has to be parallel. This simple rule must not be so simple because so many students just can't seem to get it right. Let's break it down. What elements of a sentence can have the same function?

Items in a Series

"The participants were women, over 21, and had red hair." The items in this series should all be nouns, all be adjectival phrases, or all be verb phrases, not all three. For example: "Participants were red-headed women over age 21." (This sentence no longer contains a series.) Another example: "Participants were female, aged 21 or over, and red-headed." (This sentence contains a series of adjectives.)

Exercise 1

Find examples of parallelism in series. Underline the parallel words.

Find the answer using InfoTrac College Edition (second paragraph): Friedland, D. S., & Price, R. H. (2003). Underemployment: Consequences for the health and well-being of workers. *American Journal of Community Psychology, 32,* 33–45.

1. These included <u>eating</u> plums, <u>preparing</u> simple meals with plums, <u>researching</u> plums, <u>selling</u> plums, <u>buying</u> plums, and <u>growing</u> high-quality plums.

2. Low self-esteem is characterized by <u>paranoia</u> concerning bad hair, <u>obsession</u> with ring around the collar, and <u>unwillingness</u> to engage in violent confrontations.

3. _____

   _____

4. _____

   _____

5. _____

_____

Verb Forms

Verb forms must be parallel when they are joined in a series or by any kind of connecting word. There is an error in this sentence: "Participants were left alone and were being watched through a two-way mirror." *Were left alone* is not parallel to *were being watched*. Correct it this way: "Participants were left alone and were watched . . ."

Another example: "Dogs are more influential than cats, thereby occupying more leadership positions." *Are* is the third person plural present tense form of the verb; it is not parallel to *-ing*. Correct the sentence this way: "Dogs are more influential than cats, and therefore they occupy more leadership positions." *Occupy* is a third person plural present form.

Another one: "Participants were asked to read, and they evaluated the stories." Both verbs should be passive or both should be active: "Participants were asked to read and evaluate the stories."

Exercise 2

Find examples of parallel verb forms with conjunctions or with series.

Find the answer using InfoTrac College Edition (paragraph 8): Trentham, S., & Larwood, L. (2001). Power and gender influences on responsibility attributions: The case of disagreements in relationships. *The Journal of Social Psychology, 141,* 730–751.

1. Participants completed a questionnaire for the first 5 minutes, banged their heads on a wall for the next 5 minutes, and completed a second questionnaire in the final 5 minutes.

2. The psychology majors were praised and were given candy by the dean.

3. _____

_____

4. _____

_____

Half-Empty Comparisons

More likely than what? Older than whom? This rule will keep you from writing sentences that can be ambiguous. If you are using the comparative form of an adjective (the *-er* form, such as older, faster, or better), be sure that the reader knows which two items are being compared. In conversation, this is usually not a problem. If you say, "It's more likely to rain today," your listener knows whether you mean more likely than it is to snow or more likely than it is to rain tomorrow. Sometimes when you are writing, however, it is hard to remember that your reader is not as well informed about your context or your motives as your listener might be in conversation. So when you write that the experimental group performed better on the posttest, for example, your reader does not know if that means better than on the pretest or better than the control group performed on the posttest. It is perfectly acceptable to write, "The experimental group performed better on the posttest than the control group did," or "The experimental group performed better on the posttest than on the pretest." On one of your drafts, read through just looking for comparatives, and make sure they are unambiguous.

Another potential problem with comparisons is the failure to make the second part completely clear. This violation results in a sentence like this: "Participants rated the soda in the paper cups higher than the plastic." Did they like the soda better than the plastic?

Exercise 3

Find sentences that contain comparisons.

 Find the answer using InfoTrac College Edition (second paragraph): Lippa, R. A. (2003). Handedness, sexual orientation, and gender-related personality traits in men and women. *Archives of Sexual Behavior, 32,* 103–114.

1. Participants associated more positive emotions with the photographs of the house than with those of the elephant.

2. _____

_____

3. _____

_____

4. _____

_____

Agreement Between Subject and Verb

Subject–verb agreement is typically a problem only when a lot of words intervene between the subject and verb. When that happens, there is a tendency to allow the verb to agree in number with whatever noun is nearby and feels like the main topic of the sentence, even though that noun is not strictly the grammatical subject of the verb.

Exercise 4

Find a long sentence that really only has one subject and one verb. Underline the subject and the verb.

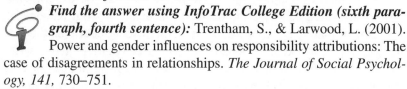 *Find the answer using InfoTrac College Edition (sixth paragraph, fourth sentence):* Trentham, S., & Larwood, L. (2001). Power and gender influences on responsibility attributions: The case of disagreements in relationships. *The Journal of Social Psychology, 141,* 730–751.

1. The goal of all but a few (and those few were the only naturalistic experiments ever conducted on communication between humans and mole rats) of Smith's studies was unfathomable.

2. The objectives of the study, albeit obscure and perhaps not amenable to unbiased interpretation by all but a few highly educated psychology students, as was common similarly in the research of Casteneda, were altruistic.

3. The unrealistic nature of the participants' responses to the frightening scenarios was surprising.

4. _____

   _____

   _____

Agreement Between Noun and Pronoun

Students come to college knowing that pronouns must "agree" in number with the nouns to which they refer. However, in writing psychology papers, students often fail to achieve perfect agreement between nouns and pronouns. The problem is most frequent with the possessive *their.* One cause is the effort to use the nonsexist phrase *he or she* as the subject of the sentence and then later referring to *their* left hand, for example. Remember also that *or* signifies a singular, not a plural, situation. The same goes for *each* (each person *cannot* use *their* pencil). This type of error is so common that you should give your paper a read-through just to check every *their* against its referent. The solution will usually be to choose a plural form for the sentence subject, and then use all the plural pronouns you like afterward.

The problem also arises in the following construction: "When a child becomes aggressive, they often need a nap." The author of this sentence has mixed up *a child* and *they,* and then gone on to compound the damage by allowing all these children only one nap. Are they sharing the same nap? Here are some ways out: "Naps often help when children have become aggressive." "When a child becomes aggressive, put that child to sleep for a nap." "When a child becomes aggressive, he or she needs a nap."

Exercise 5

Find some sentences with pronouns. Underline the pronoun and the noun to which it refers.

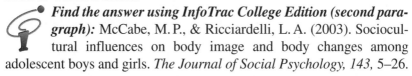 ***Find the answer using InfoTrac College Edition (second paragraph):*** McCabe, M. P., & Ricciardelli, L. A. (2003). Sociocultural influences on body image and body changes among adolescent boys and girls. *The Journal of Social Psychology, 143,* 5–26.

1. We isolated <u>participants</u> by placing <u>them</u> in cardboard boxes.

2. Freud emphasized the <u>individual's</u> need for soft drinks as well as <u>his or her</u> confrontation with sexuality.

3. _____

   _____

4. _____

   _____

Run-On Sentence or Comma Splice

To understand once and for all how to avoid run-on sentences, you will have to back up and understand once and for all what an independent clause is. A *clause* is a group of related words containing a subject and a predicate. An *independent clause* makes complete sense and is just like a sentence. A *dependent clause* also contains a subject and a predicate, but it begins with a word that ruins the whole prospect of looking like a sentence. It doesn't make complete sense because that little introductory word *depends* on another part of the sentence to make sense.

Independent clause: The participants ate the sausages.

Dependent clause: Although the participants ate the sausages

You may not join two independent clauses with a comma. (If you do, you have written a run-on sentence or a comma splice.) For example: "The participants ate the sausages, the experimenter watched." (Run-on sentence.)

To correct the situation you have three choices: (a) make two sentences by trading the comma for a period; (b) trade the comma for a semicolon—after all, something made you think these two sentences felt like one; or (c) join the two with a *coordinating conjunction.* Memorize the list of coordinating conjunctions now:

and   but   for   nor   or   so   yet   whereas

Getting back to the original problem, here are some solutions:

The participants ate the sausages; the experimenter watched.

The participants ate the sausages. The experimenter watched.

The participants ate the sausages, and the experimenter watched.

Exercise 6

Find some examples of sentences with two independent clauses joined by a coordinating conjunction.

Find the answer using InfoTrac College Edition (first paragraph): Brewer, N. T., & Chapman, G. B. (2003). Contrast effects in judgments of health hazards. *The Journal of Social Psychology, 143,* 341–354.

1. We instructed participants to sit comfortably, yet no chairs were provided.

2. These results show no relationship between gender and hair length, but they support the results of previous studies.

3. _____

_____

4. _____

_____

The other way to get into trouble with a run-on sentence is to join two independent clauses with the wrong kind of conjunctive word: a *conjunctive adverb.* Here is an example: "The participants ate the sausages, however, the experimenters never saw a thing." *However* is one of the words (conjunctive adverb) that cannot legally join two independent clauses. When you find one of these run-ons in your work, make two sentences out of it: "The participants ate the sausages. However, the experimenters never saw a thing."

Here is a list of conjunctive adverbs that are likely to get you into this type of trouble:

afterward	also	besides	consequently
furthermore	however	indeed	later
likewise	moreover	nevertheless	otherwise
similarly	then	therefore	thus

Notice what lovely words they are when they begin sentences. Use them whenever you can. Just don't use them to join two independent clauses.

Colons With Lists

Sometimes a colon introduces a list. Some students use a colon to introduce every list. However, if you have a word or phrase that indicates that a list is on its way, use a comma instead. These are some common examples:

for example	for instance	namely	that is

The exception to this rule is *as follows* or *the following.* These list-introducing phrases *do* take a colon. Another exception is *such as.* That one has *no* punctuation before the list.

Sometimes a list just serves as the object of a verb: "The participants touched turtles, snakes, lizards, and jellyfish." If you are the kind of person who puts a colon after the word *touched* in that sentence, stop it.

If it sounds as if most lists need no colons, it sounds about right. The only really good time to use a colon (other than with *as follows*) is when an entire sentence (or independent clause) introduces the list.

Exercise 7

Find examples of colon usage with lists.

 Find the answer using InfoTrac College Edition (second paragraph): Rotenberg, K.J., & Sullivan, C. (2003). Children's use of gaze and limb movement cues to infer deception. *Journal of Genetic Psychology, 164,* 175–187.

1. There were three conditions: turtle scenario, snake scenario, and lizard scenario.

2. The experimenter gave these instructions: Complete the questionnaire and draw a birthday cake on the back of each page.

3. _____

   _____

4. _____

   _____

Comma Before and (and Sometimes or)

Some students use a mistaken rule that looks like this: Use a comma before every *and,* and while you're at it, every *or.* This is probably the result of overlearning this rule: Use a comma before the *and* that coordinates two independent clauses (actually, before any of the coordinating conjunctions). Or this one: Use a comma before the *and* (and *or*) that signals the last item in a series.

But there is no comma allowed before the *and* in the compound subject or compound predicate (unless there is a series longer than two—if so, use the series rule for commas). Here is an example of this error: "The participants read every fourth word, and ate every third olive." No comma is allowed in that sentence—take it out: "The participants read every fourth word and ate every third olive." That *and* simply joins the two parts of a compound predicate. Without the nonsense, it just says they read and ate. You would never put a comma in if that's all there were: "They read and ate."

The same goes for a compound subject: "The fourth-grade boys with shoes, and the third-grade girls with hats traded insults." That comma is illegal—take it out. It merely joins the two parts of a compound subject: "The boys and girls traded insults." When you think you need a comma before a coordinating conjunction, find the bare bones of the sentence—the single-word subject, verb, and object—and see how the comma feels. If it still feels good, do it.

Exercise 8

Find sentences with very wordy compound subjects, predicates, and objects. Notice that they do not have commas—unless the compound is of three or more items, of course.

Find the answer using InfoTrac College Edition (first paragraph): Lawson, A. E. (2002). The origin of conditional logic: Does a cheater detection module exist? *Journal of Genetic Psychology, 163,* 425–444.

1. This startling claim was supported by a statistical analysis that failed to find a significant direct relation between age and ability to dance the tango but did find significant relationships between age and a positive view of tango dancers and between a positive view of tango dancers and ability to tango.

2. This is assessed by a decrease in heart rate and/or an increase in vigilance in response to pushes and shoves as a consequence of prior exposure to pushes and shoves.

3. _____

   _____

   _____

Comma When You Need a Breath

It's easy to see why someone might be tempted to use a comma when sentence parts get very long: You need a breath. However, needing a breath is an absolutely illegal use of the comma. If that is really the only reason you can think of, don't do it. Sometimes this mistake results in the placement of a comma between the subject and the predicate— something no one would do on purpose.

Exercise 9

Read the sentences from the previous exercise aloud. Even though they have no commas, feel free to take a breath while saying them.

Important Differences Between People and Things

The relative pronoun *who* is for people. You may never use anything else. This sentence contains a common mistake: "The participants that were in the first group rode horses." If participants are people, use *who* instead of *that*.

Exercise 10

Find sentences with people referred to by the relative pronoun *who*.

Find the answer using InfoTrac College Edition (first paragraph): Dishon-Berkovits, M., & Koslowsky, M. (2002). Determinants of employee punctuality. *The Journal of Social Psychology, 142,* 723–739.

1. Individuals who went to bed early were likely to wake up wealthier and wiser than those who went to bed late.

2. Participants who did not return for the second session were tarred and feathered.

3. _____

   _____

4. _____

   _____

Preparing a Poster Presentation

Many students are required to prepare a research report in the style of an APA manuscript for at least one psychology class. However, because your first professional presentation of your research is more likely to be in the form of a poster presentation, many psychology departments are encouraging students to participate in poster sessions during their undergraduate years. In some cases, this is an in-house forum for advanced psychology majors; in others, it is a requirement of the Research Methods class. There are also several regional and national undergraduate research conferences every year that feature poster presentations by students in psychology and other sciences. In addition, many students present research at state and regional psychology conventions like the Southeastern Psychological Association convention. Some of these have sessions sponsored by Psi Chi, the national honor society for psychology students, just for student posters.

What Is a Poster Session?

Research is presented in the form of a display covering a board measuring about 4 by 6 feet. The boards are arranged in rows filling the room reserved for this purpose. They may fill a room as large as a convention hall or as small as a classroom. You, the researcher, stand in front of your display, and interested persons stop, read, chat, ask questions, offer advice. This goes on for 1 to 2 hours.

Presenting a poster has advantages over presenting a talk. For one thing, it is less frightening. For another, only people who really have an interest in your work are paying attention, and you have their full attention. You may come away with ideas for how to improve your next study or how the current data could be better presented. The observer can ask questions and spend as little or as much time with a presentation as he or she wants. The disadvantage is that it requires some serious planning to make the presentation as reader friendly as possible in this type of situation. People will be standing up, distracted by a lot of ambient noise, and unsure how much time to commit to any given poster in light of those that remain to be seen. If you develop strong empathy for the consumer's plight, it will help you decide what to present on your poster and how to display it.

Even though poster presentations are becoming increasingly popular for disseminating research findings, the *Publication Manual* provides no guidance for preparing one. What, then, do authors rely on for poster rules? First, when a poster is accepted for presentation, presenters are usually provided with very brief guidelines from the organization sponsoring the conference. These generally include: (a) the size of the display area each author will have; (b) the suggestion that the poster should be readable from a distance of about 3 feet (with the lettering for title, author, and affiliation at least 1 inch high and the rest at least 3.8 inches high); and (c) a diagram of possible arrangements of title, abstract, introduction, method, results, and conclusions.

▲ **REMINDER BOX** ▼

Your poster must be readable from a distance of 3 feet.

Although these are useful guidelines, the second method for learning how to present your findings in poster format is even more effective: Go to a poster session. You will see that there are limitless ways to follow the general rules conference organizers provide, and you may even see that some people have ignored the rules completely. You will quickly learn, for example, that the rule about the font being legible from a distance is not a good one to break because no one seems tempted to read the posters with small print. Students in or near major metropolitan areas may have the opportunity to attend a national or regional psychology meeting. If your university has an annual forum of some type, don't miss it. Or perhaps a neighboring university has conferences you can attend.

You are not bound by APA style—only by the spirit of the style. That means that you must be clear, fair to those whose work came before yours, and intellectually honest about the positive and negative sides of what you have done. But it also means that you do not need to follow a rigid format. You can use numbered lists or bulleted points instead of paragraphs, for example. You can use tables or circles and arrows to illustrate your theories or research design.

▲ REMINDER BOX ▼
Posters are true to the spirit of APA format, but the rules of presentation are relaxed.

Preparing the Poster

Use the same abstract that you prepared for your written research report. This is the only section that can remain unchanged.

The introduction will have to be very different from the one you prepared for the written report. You have to include the purpose and significance of your topic and your hypotheses, but you must reduce the literature review considerably. Here are some ways to highlight relevant literature:

- Discuss the first study to address your topic in its current form. Then describe a very relevant recent one, especially if you are replicating and extending it. There may be more than one very similar to yours; mention several of the most similar.

- Discuss the competing theoretical positions surrounding your work. Then describe the study that most closely resembles your method.

- Provide a general explanation without references about how this problem has been addressed traditionally in research. Then explain, with references if appropriate, how you will diverge from this tradition and why.

Keep the introduction as short as you can. Try to keep it to two or three pages of large type. Remember the distractions that the reader faces. In these situations, people may only read a part of what you have written. If there is a crucial section of the introduction that you want to be sure gets read, make it visually distinct from the rest. Do this with the tricks your computer can produce: bullets, frames, bold italics, color.

▲ REMINDER BOX ▼

Make the introduction section no longer than three large-type pages.

The Method section has the potential to attract the most attention. Decide what is the most efficient way for someone to get the feeling of what the participants experienced. You may want to post the materials themselves (or some portions of them). If you showed pictures, post the pictures. If participants read vignettes, put up a sample. If they performed a task with a piece of equipment, include a snapshot of someone using the equipment. If they made copies of drawings, put up a sample of the drawing and a sample copy. You do not have to provide the detail necessary to replicate, but you do have to provide the minimum necessary for someone to understand what you did. Of course, if you borrowed any of the details from a previous author, you should provide the references. In a brief narrative of the procedure, include enough to satisfy the reader that you did it right. That is, provide:

■ The number of participants and any important data about them

■ The design

■ A brief description of the task

■ The grouping variables

■ The nature of the control condition

▲ REMINDER BOX ▼

Consider posting parts or photos of the actual materials.

The results you post will be primarily tables and figures. You need only introduce them with a statement of the analyses you conducted and the significant findings.

Instead of a discussion, posters usually have *conclusions*. The difference is that conclusions are less speculative and more directly tied to the hypotheses and results. There is no room for implications or suggestions for future research. Conclusions can be a few numbered points that you make about the relationship between the results and the hypotheses.

▲ **REMINDER BOX** ▼

Posters usually have conclusions instead of discussion.

You will have to prepare a References section if you referred to others' work. Occasionally, you will see posters without references, but students should plan on a brief list of references.

After you have prepared a draft of your poster, try printing a page in a large font. You should experiment with a few variations and include some bold fonts. Try a landscape (sideways) orientation of the paper to see how that looks. Ask a friend to stand 3 feet back from these samples and help you decide which is easiest to read. When you are satisfied, print it all and see how much space it actually fills. Lay it out in various ways, always keeping pieces of the same section close together and putting some extra space between sections. Decide if your reader will be reading across or down, and keep the orientation consistent. Be sure the sequence is easy for the reader to understand. Number your pages or use arrows to help readers move through the material in the manner you deem appropriate.

▲ **REMINDER BOX** ▼

Make it easy for the reader to understand the sequence in which pages should be read.

If you find that you have completely filled a 4- by 6-foot space with paper, you have written too much. Don't make it too daunting for that poster session attendee who is just milling around looking for something interesting to read. If your poster has some empty space, it will have more appeal and will be more likely to be read by more people than if the board is completely filled with writing.

Experimenting with large fonts will allow you to see which areas jump out most clearly. They will likely be the tables, photos, diagrams, bulleted lists, or otherwise distinct sections. Make sure that you are happy with this effect. If someone reads only one part of the poster, it will be that part. But will that be the right part? This is the time to be sure that you have made the visually distinct areas the ones you want to be read first.

Finally, you must prepare a title banner. The type for the title, author, and affiliation must be larger than that used in the body of the poster. You can experiment with placing a title section across the center of the top or the abstract page on the top left and the title banner to the right of it. You will probably spend a lot of time arranging and rearranging the pieces.

▲ REMINDER BOX ▼
The letters in the title should be about 1 inch tall.

When you are satisfied that you have arranged just the right amount of material in the space allotted for your poster, you can think about adding the final touches of visual appeal: a piece of colored paper behind each of your sheets; section titles backed separately on colored paper; a band of color framing each page; all pages mounted on lightweight poster board; two colors versus one color framing each page. Just remember the goal of the presentation: attracting the attention of attendees at a scientific meeting who are looking for something easy on the eyes and interesting to read. Remember that you are showing off your scientist side more than your artist side at this event. Don't be tempted to spend more time on form than on substance.

It is becoming increasingly popular to use a program such as PowerPoint to prepare posters on a single sheet with a large-format printer. You do this by putting everything on a single PowerPoint slide. If you have the use of such a printer, do it this way instead of on individual sheets of paper. It is very costly, however, to have these types of posters made at businesses (like Kinko's) that do printing. It can cost over $100 in some areas to do a single poster in color. Black-and-white posters are not expensive to produce and can often be done for under $10.

Finally, reduce the contents of your poster back to a 10- or 12-point font and reproduce it for handouts. Conference organizers often suggest how many to prepare. If this is an in-house function, your instructor will guide you. People who browse posters expect to have a hard copy available to take home for future reference. Be sure to include your address and e-mail address on the title page.

Preparing Yourself

What will actually happen at the poster session is that strangers will walk up to your poster, give it a glance, and do one of three things:

1. Walk away.

2. Read it.

3. Talk to you.

If they walk away, you feel rejected. No one can adequately prepare for that. But be aware that people have different interests, and the topic of your poster is not on everyone's "A list." If they read it, you wonder what to do with yourself while this is happening. Again, until it happens, you can't know how to prepare. But if they talk to you, you *can* be prepared. That is because they always say approximately the same thing: "Tell me the quick version of what you did." You went to all the trouble of making it artistic, easy to read, self-standing. Yet this lazy stranger wants you to tell it? Shocking! But you can be ready with the speech you have prepared. Go for the visual space that you have designed to stand out—point to it and give your already prepared quick oral version. If this is an in-house event or an undergraduate meeting for the sciences in general, you may have nonpsychologists in attendance. Prepare a version in lay terms. If this is a professional meeting for psychologists, prepare a version intended for general psychologists.

Finally, here is advice from my own Research Methods class. After the students presented posters for the first time, I asked what would be the single most important piece of advice they would give to next year's class. Their answer? Eat lunch first and wear comfortable shoes!

Wrapping It Up

You are probably not surprised to learn that after you have written the first draft of your paper, you still have work to do. But the worst is over, so give yourself a moment to enjoy that feeling. I have called this section of the book "Wrapping It Up" because the phrase has two meanings. Think of the rewriting and editing you do after the first draft in two ways: (a) you will now finish up your project and (b) you will do what is necessary to make it an appealing package.

Students sometimes call this job "proofreading," but that is not the correct word. It makes it sound as if after your first draft all you have to do is check it over for typos and spelling errors. That is what you do with the last draft, which is a bit farther down the line. *First, you revise; second, you edit; third, you proofread.* Each of these may involve more than one draft.

First Rewrite

The first rewrite (resulting in the second draft) must be conceptual. This will be a long process, so save yourself a day to do it. The best idea is to finish your first draft 2 full days before it is due (assuming that you can devote a big part of those 2 days to this paper—otherwise, allow extra days). In this rewrite you will not give style a thought.

Introduction

Think through your sequencing of paragraphs. Try to remember what your purpose was for each one, and now review the order to see if it is correct. Make sure you have all the pieces of your argument in place. Check to make sure that you have included the following:

■ The purpose of your study

■ Why it is important

■ Hypotheses or research questions

■ Rationales for hypotheses

■ General information about method

■ Definitions of variables

Look for paragraphs with only one or two sentences. If you find any, fix them now. Either elaborate on what you have written, move the material to a more logical place, or remove those sentences.

Now try to outline your paper. Outline what is really there and not what you meant to write. Step back and see if that outline is the best possible organization of your source material. If you see whole paragraphs in the wrong place, move them. After they have been moved, make sure transitions still work, or change them. If you see gaps where something should be explained or fleshed out, do it.

Check your subheadings. See if they still work now that you have made some changes. Can you improve on them? If you have not used subheadings, consider putting some in now.

Method

First, look over your subheadings and confirm they accurately describe the material in each section. Next, examine the information you provide about participants. Check to make sure that you have reported

■ Age and gender

■ Type of population they represent (e.g., first-year psychology students)

■ Compensation they received for participating

■ How many did not complete the experiment and why

■ Appropriate demographic information for each group (if applicable)

If you used an *apparatus,* check to make sure that you

- Provided enough information for replication
- Made it clear what experience participants had while using it
- Indicated how someone could buy or build it

If you have a special section for *materials,* does it stand alone or depend on information about conditions? If it makes no sense to someone as yet unfamiliar with your conditions, reorganize now. If you have used materials created by someone else, check to make sure that you have included the appropriate reference. If you have created your own materials, have you provided examples? Is there enough information to replicate?

Look at the *procedure.* Try very hard to put yourself in the shoes of someone who wasn't there. Are there any sentences that wouldn't make sense for that person? If so, they are not necessarily bad sentences; more likely, they are in the wrong place. The best thing would be to try this section out on a friend. As you read it aloud, watch that person's face. If you notice a funny look, you have skipped some information that someone needs in order to put the pieces together clearly. Alternatively, have the friend read the section aloud to you.

Check to make sure that you have

- Done a good job conveying the instructions you gave to participants
- Provided enough information to replicate
- Included instructions on scoring (if applicable)

Results

Look at your original data analysis. Make sure that every analysis that should be in your paper is there. Double-check *every* number against the printout from the statistics package you used or against the math that you did. This is also a good time to make sure that letters used in reporting statistics (e.g., t, n, F, p) are italicized (but not the Greek letters).

If you have used tables or figures to display data, every one should be mentioned in this section. There should be enough information in the text to allow the reader to know what types of data are in the tables and figures. Also, the relevant means and percentages should be either in the text or in tables (or figures), but not in both places.

Discussion

With your introduction on one side and your discussion on the other, check to make sure that every hypothesis or question mentioned in one is mentioned in the other. Next, with your results on one side and your discussion on the other, do the same thing.

Now outline your Discussion section. If you have only topics and no subtopics in your outline, you may have restated your results without discussing them. Remember your options:

- Similarities between your findings and someone else's
- Differences between your findings and someone else's
- Relationship between these findings and theories mentioned in your introduction
- Alternative explanations for the findings
- Suggested explanations for negative results
- Limitations of the study
- Implications of the findings
- Practical applications
- Suggestions for further research (with rationales)

References

This is a good time to check your references. Every reference in your paper should be on your references list and vice versa. Check the spellings while you are at it; your spell-checker won't pick up errors in people's names.

Abstract

The last part of the first rewrite is checking the abstract. Assuming that you worked pretty hard to get it right the first time, you have only to double-check at this point to make sure that any changes you have made in the body of the paper do not affect the abstract. If you are still happy with it, move on to the next part of the wrap-up.

Second Rewrite

With your major revisions behind you, it is time to concentrate on style. Now you will see if you can tighten up your organization at the paragraph level and make sure your sentences are clean.

Begin with the paragraphs. Does each one start with a topic sentence? Is there something about that sentence that makes it clear why the paragraph is located where it is? For example, is there a subheading nearby that makes the reader expect such a topic? Is there a transition word that relates to the previous paragraph? Remember, you have a list in Chapter 2—use it. Finally, does every sentence in that paragraph relate to the topic?

You are probably sick of the paper by now, but that is to be expected. You will learn to love this paper again before you hand it in because it will be a really attractive package. After all, you have just put on the wrapping paper and taped it closed. Still, some of the tape may be missing, and you haven't tied it up in a ribbon yet.

Now you have to check every sentence for gross errors. First, make sure each sentence is really a sentence—not a run-on or a fragment. Next, find the grammatical subject of every sentence and underline it. Then, make sure the verb is appropriate in number. While you are at it, make sure the verb defines an action that is logically possible for the subject. For example, if you have written that an experiment *tried* to do something, now is the time to reconsider. Think about misplaced modifiers at this time. Admittedly, misplaced modifiers are not easy to spot in one's own work, but sometimes when you are studying your sentences this closely, you can spot them.

This is also the time to check for errors in parallel construction. These, too, can be hard to spot; look especially at items in a series, compound verbs, and phrases containing comparisons.

Now your package is securely covered in paper that won't come off. No untrimmed edges are showing.

Third Inspection—Not a Rewrite

You are nearing the home stretch—preparing to put a ribbon on that package. Pass your eyes over your paper again. Circle the commas and colons. Try to remind yourself of the rule you learned in school or in this book that prescribes that punctuation mark in that place. You should have a grammar book somewhere on your desk; perhaps you can find that rule. If you can't specify the rule, you should seriously consider omitting the punctuation mark. Most of what is left can be streamlined with the use of the search function on your word processor. If you are not familiar yet with this function, take some time now to figure out how to *find* or *search* for a word or phrase. Also, it is a good idea to figure out the command that takes you to the top of your document because it will be efficient to return there after each search. When you are ready, search and correct if necessary:

- *Apostrophe:* For each one, if it is used in a contraction, change the contraction to a more formal phrase. If it is a simple plural with no possession intended, omit the apostrophe. If the intention is possessive, but the word is a pronoun, omit the apostrophe. If it is a possessive noun, note whether it is singular or plural and make sure the apostrophe is in the right place.

- *Their:* First, make sure you didn't mean to write *there.* When that is taken care of, check to make sure that the noun referred to is apparent to the reader and that it is plural. Then do a search for *there* just to make sure you didn't mean to write *their.*

- *Feel, felt, think, thought, believe, believed, said, state, stated, prove,* and *proved:* If these refer to the activities of researchers you have cited, think it over. Perhaps you should substitute one of the words on your list of researcher verbs in Chapter 2.

- *Current* and *present:* Do not use these words to refer to experiments other than yours.

- *Data, hypotheses, hypothesis, stimulus, stimuli, analysis, analyses, phenomena, phenomenon, criteria,* and *criterion:* There is always a danger that the verbs in these sentences might not agree in number with these nouns.

- *Since* and *while:* Remember, the *Publication Manual* specifies that these words are only used in their temporal sense. You may need to substitute *because* and *whereas* if they are more accurate.

- *Between* and *among:* Use *between* for two things, *among* for more than two.

- *You* and *we:* Unless you are quoting instructions to participants, rephrase without these words.

- *Quotation marks:* Try one more time to paraphrase instead of quote.

- *Non, pre, post,* and *sub:* These are not words. They have to be attached to other words.

■ Ampersands should appear in parentheses. Authors' names are joined by *and* outside of parentheses.

■ *Latin abbreviations:* Make sure they are punctuated correctly and that they appear only in parentheses. See the final section of Chapter 2 if you need a refresher.

Now you can run your spell-checker. It won't help you with names, so look them over each time the spell-checker finds them. Check the spelling yourself.

Final Touches

You have only one task left. Read your paper aloud. Read every word you have written. This is the way you will notice whether you have left little words out or put extra ones in. All writers have trouble seeing dumb little mistakes because we know what something is supposed to say. Cognitive psychologists call this "top-down" processing. Our minds are working with meaning, and sometimes our eyes miss the details.

This is the time when you begin to feel proud of your work; you are not feeling as sick of it as you were by the second revision. This is because you can appreciate how many little improvements you made even after you thought you were finished. You can finally take this paper out in public (or hand it in to your professor), and it will surely make a good impression.

References

American Psychological Association (2001). *Publication manual of the American Psychological Association* (5th ed.). Washington, DC: Author.

American Psychological Association (2001, January 10). *Electronic reference formats recommended by the American Psychological Association.* Washington, DC: Author. Retrieved November 15, 2003 from the World Wide Web: http://www.apastyle.org/elecref.html

Bem, D. J. (1995). Writing a review article for Psychological Bulletin. *Psychological Bulletin, 118,* 172–177.

Nicol, A. A. M., & Pexman, P. M. (2003). *Displaying your findings: A practical guide for creating figures, posters, and presentations.* Washington, DC: American Psychological Association.

Nicol, A. A. M., & Pexman, P. M. (1999). *Presenting your findings: A practical guide for creating tables.* Washington, DC: American Psychological Association.

Rimer, S. (2003, September 3). A campus fad that's being copied: Internet plagiarism seems on the rise. [Internet version]. http://www.nytimes.com

Talub, R. S. (2000). Copyright, plagiarism, and Internet-based research projects: Three "golden rules." *Tech Trends, 44* (4), 7–9.

Index

TO THE OWNER OF THIS BOOK:

I hope that you have found *Writing With Style: APA Style Made Easy,* Third Edition, useful. So that this book can be improved in a future edition, would you take the time to complete this sheet and return it? Thank you.

School and address: _____

_____

Department: _____

Instructor's name:_____

1. What I like most about this book is:_____

_____

_____

2. What I like least about this book is:_____

_____

_____

3. My general reaction to this book is:_____

_____

_____

4. The name of the course in which I used this book is:_____

_____

5. Were all of the chapters of the book assigned for you to read? _____

   If not, which ones weren't?_____

6. In the space below, or on a separate sheet of paper, please write specific suggestions for improving this book and anything else you'd care to share about your experience in using this book.

_____

_____

FOLD HERE

BUSINESS REPLY MAIL
FIRST-CLASS MAIL   PERMIT NO. 34   BELMONT CA

POSTAGE WILL BE PAID BY ADDRESSEE

Attn: Psychology/Vicki Knight

Wadsworth/Thomson Learning
10 Davis Drive
Belmont, CA   94002-9801

FOLD HERE

OPTIONAL:

Your name:_____ Date: _____

May we quote you, either in promotion for *Writing With Style: APA Style Made Easy,* Third Edition, or in future publishing ventures?

Yes: _____ No: _____

Sincerely yours,

Lenore T. Szuchman